A stimulus causes response or incites .... *Bible-Based Spiritual Stimulus Plan* does both. Dr. Johnson shows himself to be a poet, prophet, and pastor who can stir the soul toward living victoriously. By creatively weaving humor, candor, and wisdom, he simultaneously corrects us and encourages us to live disciplined, authentic, compassionate, and missional lives. Biblical, theological, lyrical, and practical, this book will call readers to visit it again and again. And each read will empower you afresh.

—**David Emmanuel Goatley**
Executive Secretary-Treasurer
Lott Carey Baptist Foreign Mission Convention
Washington, DC

Clearly written, easily read, divinely inspired! Dr. Cureton L. Johnson shares the story of his life and the long-term strategy to discern and stimulate fulfillment of God's desires for your life. While the political parties debate the approaches to stimulate our nation's economy, few readers will dispute the value of Dr. Johnson's scripture-based stimulus plan for life.

—**Justice Patricia Timmons-Goodson**
Supreme Court of North Carolina

A new decade is upon us and with it comes new opportunities for the people of God to dream dreams and see visions. Dr. Cureton L. Johnson's spiritual stimulus plan is an inviting and informative set of real life situations linking biblical principles, reflection questions, and contemporary applications for the living of these days. Christian believers everywhere will find throughout these pages wellsprings of accessible spiritual wisdom to meet and overcome life's complex and sometimes overwhelming challenges.

—**Alton B. Pollard, III, Ph.D.**
Dean, Howard University School of Divinity

Like the fine pastor/preacher and PK (preacher's kid) that he is, Dr. Cureton L. Johnson has undoubtedly made his late father and grandfather proud! He has provided the body of Christ with a timely, inspirational, and practical guide to navigating the next decade. Readers will readily relate to his freshly-written and easily-recognizable personal accounts; students of the Word will enjoy the many contemporary analogies; and churches everywhere can rejoice that there is—at long last—an accessible, purposeful, and biblical stimulus plan for the people of God!

—**Rev. Dr. Timothy Tee Boddie**, Pastor
Friendship Baptist Church, Atlanta, GA
Immediate Past Executive Secretary of
the Hampton University Ministers' Conference

Cureton Johnson's wise, Bible-based reflections challenge us to be prophets of a new time—one filled with Spirit-led hope and change, especially for those on the margins of society. He urges us to speak to our elected leaders, to transform our faith communities, and to act as gifted, stimulated people of God, endowed with "Holy DNA." His stories—well-told and compelling—spark our courage and provide practical ways to be trusting, enduring disciples.

—**Larry Hollar**
Regional Organizer, Bread for the World,
and editor, "Hunger for the Word" Scripture series

From the caiman-infested waters of Guyana to the equally perilous waters of everyday life, the Rev. Johnson reminds us where our help, our courage, our hope come from. Chock full of practical challenges and faith-enhancing applications, his book is certain to be kept at the bedside table with a pencil close by for jotting down notes in the margins.

—**Kim Hasty**
Community News Editor, The Fayetteville Observer

BIBLE-BASED SPIRITUAL STIMULUS PLAN

BIBLE-BASED SPIRITUAL STIMULUS PLAN

12 STRIDES

TO VICTORY

IN A

NEW DECADE

CURETON L. JOHNSON

Pleasant Word™
A Division of WinePress Group™

Pleasant Word (a division of WinePress Publishing, PO Box 428, Enumclaw, WA 98022) functions only as book publisher. As such, the ultimate design, content, editorial accuracy, and views expressed or implied in this work are those of the author.

Unless otherwise noted, all Scriptures are taken from the *Holy Bible, New International Version®, NIV®*. Copyright © 1973, 1978, 1984 by Biblica, Inc.™ Used by permission of Zondervan. All rights reserved worldwide. WWW.ZONDERVAN.COM

Scripture references marked KJV are taken from the *King James Version* of the Bible.

Scripture references marked NASB are taken from the *New American Standard Bible,* © 1960, 1963, 1968, 1971, 1972, 1973, 1975, 1977 by The Lockman Foundation. Used by permission.

ISBN 13: 978-1-4141-1503-0
ISBN 10: 1-4141-1503-2
Library of Congress Catalog Card Number: 2009905732

To my father, Rev. Dr. Paul H. Johnson, Sr.; my mother, Susie C. Johnson; my mother-in-law, Annie H. Goode; my wife, Lena G. Johnson; my sons, Paul L. and Cureton M. Johnson; my sisters and brother, Delcie V. Cooke, Nita C. Byrd, and Paul H. Johnson, Jr. (their spouses and progeny); the Johnson and Cureton clans.

CONTENTS

ACKNOWLEDGMENTS

GLORY TO GOD for a daily outpouring of the Holy Spirit during the early morning hours of 2009 and 2010. Morning by morning new mercies I experienced! I am very appreciative to my book endorsers and to these very special people for their assistance: Dr. James Ashmore, professor of Old Testament Studies, Shaw University Divinity School; Nita C. Byrd, graduate student, Duke Divinity School; Edithe B. McLean, Ruth Smith, and Theresa Williams, readers; Tammy Hopf, Mary McNeil, and the Pleasant Word/Winepress staff; and the leaders of the Blue Ridge Mountains Christian Writers Conference.

I thank my 200 prayer partners and supporters who kept me lifted up during this book project. Deep gratitude is extended to the members of the First Baptist Church-Moore Street in Fayetteville, N.C., who patiently and lovingly encouraged my work.

Especially, I praise God for my extraordinary wife Lena, the love of my life. She was so wonderfully patient, helpful, encouraging, and supportive during my year of writing. She never gave up on me throughout the entire process.

INTRODUCTION
SHARE THE LIGHT

Then God said, "Let there be light," and there was light.
God saw that the light was good.
—Genesis 1:3-4

I N THE PHYSICAL realm, light stimulates photosynthesis, growth in plants, tanning of the human skin, and visibility for the human eye. Spiritually, light is the glorious presence and knowledge of God that illuminates and stimulates our personal character. It activates authentic Christian living.

The Bible-Based Spiritual Stimulus Plan (The Plan) is a book of encouragement for men and women pursuing the abundant life found in following Jesus Christ. It shines the light of the Good News (the gospel) of Jesus Christ upon our hearts and minds and fashions us into God's masterpieces for good in society. Because so many people prefer darkness to spiritual illumination, there just are not enough Christian lights in our world. Massive moral and spiritual power failures proliferate in America and must be offset by millions of points of light provided by everyday gifted Christians. People of God must step up and stimulate our nation toward new levels of excellence.

Many people have argued about the effectiveness of recent economic stimuli while too many Americans have overlooked God's *spiritual stimulus plan* revealed in Scripture. This divine stimulus was created from the foundation of the world by our Creator for the enrichment and hope of all humanity. It has successfully withstood the test of time. *The Plan* emboldens God's people to change the world by sharing the great light of God's eternal wisdom with their family, friends, and acquaintances.

The Bible informs us that "in him was life, and that life was the light of men" (John 1:4). Jesus Christ is the light of the people of the world. The Lord promised his disciples that they would "never walk in the darkness, but will have the light of life" (John 8:12). He told them, "Let your light shine before men, that they may see your good deeds and praise your Father in heaven" (Matt. 5:16). Christians are to share the light of Christ's great love and not keep it to ourselves.

Think about some of the great people of faith who have tremendously influenced the world. Mother Teresa, Billy Graham, Martin Luther King, Jr., Desmond Tutu, Howard Thurman, Dietrich Bonhoeffer, Vashti M. McKenzie, Pope John Paul II, Gardner C. Taylor, Rick Warren, and T.D. Jakes come to my mind. Yet, everyday people of God, who labor in relative obscurity are quite essential to spiritual vitality in our swiftly changing world. Our spiritual light can be brightened to more positively stimulate people in our homes, neighborhoods, towns, cities, or rural areas. The grunt and gut-check work of ministry not only takes place on the large stages of the world, but also in the thousands of small and medium-sized churches of our great land.

Some people are tempted to let the light of Jesus Christ shine just enough to give the appearance of a Christian witness, but that is not genuine Christian light. We must remember that we are the light of the world, and our spiritual lights must be set on a hill so that others are blessed (Matt. 5:14). This means our faith must be shared with people who are walking in darkness and lurking in the shadowy corners of society. *The Plan* offers biblical encouragement to guide us forward and keep us on the right road in our fast-paced communities. And it equips us to lead others toward their God—ordained destinations.

The first section of *The Plan* renews us with such basic stimuli as Alligator Courage, Prophetic Faith, Cloud Nine Hope, and Radical Love. Section two provides insider information from the Bible that shapes us into God's masterpieces. The chapters detailing these stimuli are Your Holy DNA, Spiritual Blind Dates, and Hot Tips from the BIG Bailout! Section three presents spiritual stimuli for our abundant living with the chapters Harmony Shout-Out, Kindness/Vitamin K, and Joy—A Yummy Recipe. The final section propels us on our faith journey into a new decade with two chapters, Obedience and Almighty Momentum!, and Strides to Victory and the Holy "Yet." The sermon epilogue, Be Encouraged—We Win! is taken from the Bible's book of Revelation and confirms that ultimately we will win and overcome our challenges through Jesus Christ.

All twelve stimuli include true stories, essential "Back to the Word" Bible background materials, "Go and Do Likewise" illustrations and amplifications, and practical "Outreach Ministry Activities." Challenging reflection and discussion questions fortify your group study.

God's Salvation Plan through Jesus Christ has stimulated millions of people to enjoy new spiritual life, purpose, and significance. *The Plan* encourages us to proclaim the gracious love of God to all people, and to light up the world with good deeds in Jesus' name.

From Genesis to Revelation, the Bible-Based Stimulus Plan provides vision to help you stride to victory in this new decade. Together, we can do bold new things to connect people to Jesus Christ. Remember, "if anyone is in Christ, he is a new creation; the old has gone, the new has come!" (2 Cor. 5:17).

Come on! Read *The Plan* and get spiritually stimulated to impact your world for Christ.

PART ONE

NOW ABIDE THESE THREE BASICS—PLUS ONE

ALLIGATOR COURAGE

The Lord shall preserve your going out and your coming
in from this time forth, and even forevermore.
—Psalm 121:8

AT 6:00 A.M., FIVE ministers crowded into a minibus headed to
an Amerindian church deep in the interior of Guyana, South
America (the land of many rivers). After crossing the Demerara
River, and then spending an hour bouncing and jostling over rutted
back roads, we reached the Essiquibo River. We missed the boat
(quite literally!) by just a few minutes, so our party booked rides
on two speedboats that whisked us down the river in forty-five
minutes.

At the next dock, we boarded another minibus. By now the sun
had burned away the morning mist, and the tropical heat began
testing our endurance. After another two hours along bumpy dirt
roads, with perspiration dripping from our chins and our pants
stuck to the backs of our legs, we finally reached our destination,
a small, rustic, actually dilapidated town near the Pomaroon River.
We checked into the local "hotel," an old, three-story, no-frills
house off the main dirt street. My Spartan-like room included a
bed, mosquito net, table, chair, toilet, and a small green lizard that

looked liked it might speak with a British accent while it sold me car insurance. A small fan rotated lazily as the room temperature climbed near ninety degrees. With no screens covering the open windows, insect repellant became my deodorant and cologne. After all, I was pretty sure the apostle Paul wasn't thinking about South American insects when he mentioned being a "living sacrifice."

The next evening we boarded two small speedboats to take us to the worship service at Abram's Creek Church, located on the river. We fastened life vests around our chests and fervently prayed for safety on our thirty-minute ride. Traveling with Dr. Clifford Jones, president of the Lott Carey Foreign Mission Convention, we wanted to bring encouragement to God's people in South America.

The engines revved up and the boats rose in the water as we picked up speed. The Pomaroon's blackness declared her rich soil base and thick vegetation beneath and around the waters. The skin of the indigenous people was smooth like Georgia peaches because they bathed in this mineral-rich river. As we traveled, Guyanese citizens fished, worked by the river, and tended their homes and boats. Some waved at us, for the orange life vests marked us as foreigners.

Many members of the Abrams Creek Church greeted us at the riverbank. The congregation was mostly Amerindian, the original people of Guyana. More than a hundred jammed the little church and spilled out the front door to sing, pray, and hear the Word of God. I preached from the forty-sixth Psalm, and I called my sermon "The River Inside of You." We experienced the joy of the Lord as the people sang and praised God, causing time to fly. We didn't leave until 9:30 P.M.

By now the black rainforest night covered us. Only the distant stars and a small lantern lit the way. As we began our trip—much more slowly this time—our boat's pilot cast the light of his small battery powered lantern on the water, dodging objects afloat and angling into the waves as the wind picked up and shifted directions.

Then, for a moment, he slowed the boat and pointed his light toward the shore. We saw two faint red dots reflecting from the riverbank.

"What's that?" Pastor Summers asked.

"A caiman. It's a sort of cousin to the alligator," our driver replied. Soon the caiman's eyes sank below the water like a submarine periscope.

Ten minutes later, the boatman stopped dead in the water and killed the engine. He peered into the dark night, swiveled his head side to side like a radar screen, and raised his hand for silence.

"What's wrong?" I asked. "Why are you stopping?"

"A storm is coming, a heavy rain," the boatman cautioned, artfully reading nature's warning signs. "Pull out the plastic sheeting underneath your seats and cover yourselves."

On a warm, muggy night, plastic was not my idea of proper attire. Having preached, my damp clothes stuck to me like glue. I prayed, "God help us. We're in your hands." Indeed, all five preachers (two in my boat and three in the other) began praying.

We obeyed and covered up. He started the boat and sped upstream. All was covered except my necktie, which blew wildly outside my jacket. I covered my head with a military camouflage hat and offered a brief prayer of thanks for that army officer in my church who had supplied it.

A moment later, God opened the heavens, and rain fell so hard it pelted us like blowing desert sands. The wind picked up and created waves splashing into our boat, so the pilot turned toward an Amerindian lantern-lit home onshore and drove us under a dock to shield us from the driving rain. We waited a few minutes, but it seemed like an eternity. I looked around constantly for any sign of reflecting red eyes.

"Is it safe here? What's more dangerous, the storm or the caiman?" I inquired nervously. "I don't want to be a late night snack."

"You're more than a snack," Summers joked, cracking on my six-foot, two hundred and forty pound frame.

Earlier, while we were still out in the storm, I looked up into the night sky illumined only by the spill light from the lantern. I observed rain drops dive-bombing at my face from the dark heavens above. In that moment, I began Scripture-praying (using a scripture passage as the main points of a prayer) Psalm 121:1-2: "I will lift up my eyes to the hills—from whence comes my help? My help comes from the Lord, who made heaven and earth" (NKJV). Those words filled my soul and reassured me of God's presence.

Before leaving North Carolina, I prayed that the Lord's will would be done on this trip. I knew there were dangers on any journey, yet the God of Abraham, Isaac, and Jacob would be with me. And as I came to the last verse of the psalm, the Spirit whispered, "The Lord will watch over your coming and going both now and forevermore."

I knew that no matter what happened, God was with me. I found courage amid the storm and chaos. I could not see hills as the psalmist described, yet the psalm really speaks of One beyond the hills who is able to keep us from falling and preserve us from all evil. "Yes, O Lord," my heart cried. "In you do I put my trust!"

The rains finally slowed and the winds died down. We reached the dilapidated hotel safely that night. To me, it looked more like the Ritz-Carlton.

BACK TO THE WORD: ALLIGATOR COURAGE

Remember the story of Jesus and the disciples in the storm? This is how it is described in the gospel of Matthew:

> Then he got into the boat and his disciples followed him. Without warning, a furious storm came up on the lake, so that the waves swept over the boat. But Jesus was sleeping. The disciples went and woke him, saying, "Lord, save us! We're going to drown!" He replied, "You of little faith, why are you so afraid?" Then he got up and rebuked the winds and the waves, and it was completely calm. The men were amazed and asked, "What kind of man is this? Even the winds and the waves obey him!" (8:23-27).

Even in the most trying circumstances of life, God strengthens us. When we need courage, he is our help. There is a river that runs deep within us and Jesus said, "Whoever believes in me, as the Scripture has said, streams of living water will flow from within him. By this he meant the Spirit, whom those who believed in him were later to receive" (John 7:38-39). The psalmist wrote, "There is a river whose streams make glad the city of God" (Ps. 46:4). This River sustained us on the waterways of Guyana.

Overcoming Fear

God is our help in times of trouble. But what about times of fear in our lives, the times when we are anxious and greatly concerned? These times are common to all of us. Fear erupts when we lose control and circumstances overwhelm us. What are the great fears and anxieties in your life? Is it your health, finances, marriage, job security, or some other worry? In times like these, courage is critical. We must rise above infantile milk-drinking Christian habits that sustain a weak and simple faith and never challenge us to stretch. Our faith must produce bold courage from years of chewing on the meat of Jesus' gospel. Remember, "There is no fear in love. But perfect love drives out fear, because fear has to do with punishment. The one who fears is not made perfect in love" (1 John 4:18).

Christians should be fearless people. Be fearless in advocating for the lives of the unborn and for the prosperity of children after birth. Fearless, however, does not equal foolish. Fearless does not mean killing doctors and committing violent acts in the name of Christ. Righteous courage acts against evil, but it does not become indistinguishable from the evil it detests.

Be fearless about doing the right things of God for the right reasons with the right attitudes. Be fearless in ministering to people on the streets. Be fearless in serving hungry and homeless people. Be fearless in working with youth from ungodly homes. Be fearless in opening your church doors to people who live outside the kingdom of God. Offer them a pathway to salvation.

How many poor people, if they entered your church today, would find a genuine welcome? How many unemployed persons, single parents, or prostitutes would your fellowship welcome with the transforming Word of God? Too many congregations are like country clubs, concerned only about maintaining wealth and prosperity. Would your church welcome the beaten down man or woman with HIV/AIDS into its sanctuary? Does it welcome the physically and mentally impaired? What welcome do you and your fellow church members give those who come out of our jails and prisons?

Jesus once told Peter, "...upon this rock I will build my church; and the gates of hell shall not prevail against it" (Matt. 16:18, KJV). Indeed, the church must be fearless to go into the hellholes of our communities to rescue the perishing and care for the dying. Being a Christian in a dark world requires fearless men and women willing to storm the gates of hell with a divine invasion. Jesus Christ was sent by God into the world to intrude upon the evil and darkness of sin, and to overrun humanity with divine light and goodness from heaven (John 1).

Stay in the Boat!

We didn't jump out of the boat that night on the Pomaroon River. Instead, we followed the experienced driver's instructions. He knew the river. He knew the seasons, the currents, and he knew we would be safe if we stayed in the boat. We must also stay in the boat with Jesus Christ through all of life's turmoil. As the storm worsened in Guyana, I gripped the side of the boat and sat upright, trusting the pilot who knew the sea and had been through many such storms.

Praise the Lord that we have a captain watching over our lives who has been through the storms of life. Jesus Christ came to us in the flesh and lived in a body such as ours, experiencing the pounding of life's storms. Jesus knows the waves, the tides, the weather, and the winds of life. And he has authority over all creation.

The same Jesus who sailed the Sea of Galilee sailed with us in Guyana, and that same Jesus sails with us wherever we go. He is the God who preserves our going out and our coming in. The Lord truly keeps watch over his children day and night. He never sleeps. Ever. Through sickness, pain, loss, tragedy, and challenges of all sorts, God never leaves or forsakes us.

Stay in the boat with Jesus. The Lord may not come just when we want him, but divine purpose in our lives will be accomplished if we surrender to God's grace through faith. Like Job, after we have been tested and tried, we will come forth as gold. I will say it again: Stay in the boat with Jesus.

Modern Day Pilgrims

Psalm 121 was apparently written for the pilgrims visiting Jerusalem annually to celebrate the great feasts of the Jews. Many would sing and chant as they ascended to the city and the holy temple. Their eyes could easily see the hills surrounding the Holy City. The psalmist's words remind us that God will guide and preserve us every day. The Almighty's presence is continuous.

The same God who guided the pilgrims to Jerusalem guides us modern-day pilgrims. Indeed, we cannot afford to leave our homes each day without being covered by the presence of God. Often, however, we are in such a rush to get to the next errand, the next appointment or activity that we don't stop to acknowledge God's presence and be thankful for it. In the midst of our running, we must remember the prophet Hosea, who said, "For it is time to seek the Lord, until he comes and showers righteousness on you" (10:12).

Stick Psalm 121 on your refrigerator. Let it be a constant reminder that our help comes daily from the Lord (verse two). God keeps our feet from stumbling and he never sleeps (verses three and four). God hears our cries, our pleas, and knows our needs 24/7. The Lord is our cooling system. When we are overheating, he gives us shade to recover—shade from our burdens and cover from our stresses. The Lord is an ever-present sanctuary we can enter for safety and reassurance. In the heat and passions of our daily toil, we are protected (verse six), and at night we are kept from the lunatics preying in the dark.

Every Christian experiences troubles and disturbances at times, but our souls are always preserved and constantly kept in the eternal salvation of our God. The Lord keeps and preserves our comings and goings forevermore (verse eight).

GO AND DO LIKEWISE

How can we cross over from faith to courage and do bold new things for Jesus Christ in this new decade? Like the Nike shoe slogan says, "Just Do It!" Courage is fear that has said its prayers.[1]

Many years ago a new interstate bypass was built around Richmond, Virginia. Before this, I drove through the city of Richmond on frequent trips visiting family in North Carolina and returning to Washington, D.C. On one return trip to the capital city, I took the newly constructed I-495 bypass around Richmond to save time.

A few miles up the brightly lit, six-lane superhighway stood a huge bridge over-arching a body of water. It seemingly stretched up into the clouds. A good bit afraid of heights, I could have pulled over, waited for help, or panicked and driven off the bridge into the river below. My wife slept on the passenger side, and I did not want to wimp out. Time was running out as we swiftly approached the bridge. I Scripture-prayed Psalm 121, as I did in Guyana: "The Lord will watch over your coming and going both now and forevermore." I challenged myself to believe God's words, took a deep breath, grabbed hold of Jesus and the steering wheel, and drove on.

Thank God, I have crossed that bridge without such stress dozens of times since that day. When we face huge challenges and must make difficult decisions, then we need to know—as the psalmist knew—that God is present in every condition. If we take a deep breath, grab hold of Jesus tightly, and Scripture-pray Psalm 121, we can make our decision and move on.

My experience with the I-495 bypass around Richmond ushered in new meaning for the song "I Have Decided to Follow Jesus": "I have decided to follow Jesus...no turning back, no turning back. Though no one join me, still I will follow...no turning back, no turning back. The world behind me, the cross before me...no turning back, no turning back."[2]

REFLECTION/DISCUSSION

1. How do the following Scriptures help you face the challenges in your life? "Be strong and very courageous. Be

careful to obey all the law my servant Moses gave you; do not turn from it to the right or the left, that you may be successful wherever you go" (Josh. 1:7); "He [Josiah] did what was right in the eyes of the Lord and walked in all the ways of his father David, not turning aside to the right or to the left" (2 Kings 22:2); "Do not turn aside from any of the commands I give you today, to the right or to the left, following other gods and serving them" (Deut. 28:14).

2. When I took the newly constructed I-495 bypass around Richmond, I crossed over the bridge neither looking to the right or to the left. The Scriptures above allude to a similar focus. What is the meaning of looking neither right or left when facing daunting situations?

3. What is the focus of the pilgrims in verse one of Psalm 121? Is it the hills, or the One God beyond the hills? How do you know?

4. The psalmist says, "The Lord will watch over your coming and going both now and forevermore." Do you believe this? You may not have faced a caiman in Guyana, but how has God been a powerful presence in the comings and goings of your life?

5. How do you overcome your fears? Do you turn to prayer, friends, Scripture, or therapists?

6. Read 1 John 4:18 and Psalm 27. What do these Scriptures say about fear? What is one of your favorite Scriptures to help you overcome fear?

7. Discuss the hymn, "I Have Decided to Follow Jesus," which is based on Luke 9:57. Look it up and read the words to each stanza. Does this song give you motivation and courage? Why or why not?

8. What difficult bridges (problems) has God helped you cross over in your life? From your experience, what would you recommend to others?

OUTREACH MINISTRY ACTIVITY

Choose a mission partner overseas to give your support. For example, you might meet a specific need that is beyond the scope of a missionary's monthly budget. Send needed items such as a supply of new Bibles, or an offering for medical supplies. Mission partners of the Lott Carey Foreign Mission Convention in Washington, D.C. work with poor women escaping sex trafficking, provide schools and supplies for children, provide medical assistance for the poor, and conduct many other projects globally. Contact the Lott Carey Foreign Mission Convention and channel assistance to proven missions workers on any continent in the world. Their Web site is www.lottcarey.org.

ALLIGATOR COURAGE STIMULUS SUMMARIZED

There is a river inside of you, and that River is the Holy Spirit who sustains and promotes courage.

Stay in the boat with Jesus Christ, the captain of our salvation. He has been through the storms we face, and the Lord has authority over all creation.

Stick Psalm 121 on your refrigerator or car dashboard. It is a reminder that the same God who guided the pilgrims to Jerusalem guides you today. Take courage from verse eight: "The Lord shall preserve your going out and your coming in from this time forth, and even forevermore."

When life comes at you fast, just take a deep breath, grab hold of Jesus tightly, Scripture-pray Psalm 121 (memorize it), and drive forward!

Remember, "There is no fear in love. But perfect love drives out fear" (1 John 4:18).

PROPHETIC FAITH

The righteous will live by their faith.
—Habakkuk 2:4b, NLT

IF THE OLD Testament prophet Habakkuk had lived to preach and prophesy in the southern United States during the summer of 2010, this quite possibly could be his prayer upon arising early one very warm morning to talk with God: "Well, Lord, it's gonna be another hot one today. Seems like that big red ball on the horizon is just a reminder of the burning fires in our land. Think I'll bring the dog inside by the air conditioner today. I'm troublin' you mighty early, but I just couldn't sleep much. I've got a lot on my mind.

"Maybe global warming comes from all the hot-headed passions stirred up in folks' hearts these days. Iranians died protesting in their streets. North Koreans aimed their long-range missiles at Hawaii for America's Independence Day celebration. Iraq and Afghanistan engulfed our military. More than one hundred thousand Iraqis and Americans perished in war, many of them women and children. Where does this end, O Lord?

"What do I pray for first, Lord? Our economy? Seems like you let it fall into ruins. Pardon me Lord. Sure, it's our fault—not yours. Who shall I pray for Lord? Laid-off auto workers, folks who've lost their homes, families without health insurance? And what about all the political bickering? It never ends.

"Maybe I'll pray for Michael Vick. He's out of prison after serving time for his dog fighting days. Will people forgive him? I hope he's truly repentant. Then there's Congressman Joe Wilson and Kanye West who lost their cool on TV. People can't even be civil. Forgive us, Lord, for our evil ways. And those citizens ripped off by Bernie Madoff, how despicable!

"And why must the poor suffer so much? Scores line up each week at our church food pantry. Desperate people look for clothes, rent money, medicines, and help with their utility bills. And now, folks along the Gulf Coast suffer from a massive offshore oil spill. It's so depressing.

"And what's up with this new vision you've been laying on me? It's a burden! I didn't ask you for special night 'future' vision goggles revealing all the bad stuff ahead. I'm sleepless in Carolina; can hardly get a wink. You're waking me up too early and troubling my mind. Why must I tell your folks that recovery lasts longer and hurts harder than expected, and that they'll endure protracted high unemployment rates well into this new decade? They hate that stuff, you know. Give 'em quick fixes. They're a microwave generation: instant grits, instant potatoes, instant twitter, and text messaging. Most people can't wait patiently for anything. Even church folks want sixty-minute 'shake and bake' worship services. And when I open my mouth on the sidewalk at First Community Church to say, 'Thus says the Lord,' faces grimace.

"It's a hard time to be a prophet. So why are you dumping this warn-the-people vision on me?

"OK—I hear you. Sure! You're right! Of course, you're always right. Who can argue with you? Yet, I have to ask, why do bad things happen to us when other nations seem to be more evil? Why do you use al-Qaida and Hamas and the Taliban to shame us? Violence increases all around. Corporate greed and political strife shoot up off the charts. Credit card rates hit thirty percent and more, and banks gouge people while Wall Street CEOs laugh at justice. They make up their own rules just for white-collar criminals to go free. Insurance companies mercilessly jack up their rates on working people. The rich take money to pay themselves big bonuses. CEOs put profits before people, paying themselves exorbitant salaries and taking huge bailouts. The average 'Joe' (not the plumber) hemorrhages under a pile of bills. Common hard-working laborers often suffer wage theft from bosses who don't pay up for all hours worked. Why are the scales of justice out of balance? Where's the mercy? In Jesus' name, what's your plan? How long? How long? How long O Lord?

"You're up to something! I know you are. Like giving us a black president. That surely popped our eyes out! Maybe you're reeling us in like a fisherman on his fishing line. You're pulling us out of the waters of greed, wild consumer spending, debt, and insatiable material lusts. Sure, we've got to feel some pain. Our selfish idols grew too large even for your patience: gas guzzling SUVs, oversized king cab trucks, and lavish Hummers were the last straw. You want repentance! You want changed hearts! Even church folks are guilty!

"Is your mercy on hold? Where's the bottom to all this? We're at each other's throats like Vick's fighting dogs. We daily endure contentious Birthers, Deathers, Truthers, Shouters, and Haters. When money gets tight, people turn on each other.

"Folks carry guns to political meetings, threatening violence. They paint swastikas on protest signs and speak of revolution. A man bit off his adversary's finger at a demonstration. Another man crashed an airplane into an IRS office in Texas. Where's the love? Has it vaporized? Did you not say that the righteous shall live by faith? Faith seems overwhelmed by fear. Purify us again, O Lord, and burn off the toxic stuff in our lives, the jealousy, envy, divisions, and selfishness. Replace them with faith.

"What did you say? Tell them to turn from their wicked ways? I don't know whether they'll go for that again. OK, OK, OK...I'll tell them. But remember Jeremiah. That prophet was thrown into a Jerusalem cistern centuries ago. I'll endure sacrifice, Lord, but please, not a hole in the ground. It's too hot!

"Even some preachers 'shake down' their congregations. False prophets ride in big limos with chauffeurs. Their Beamers and

Benzes fill their garages, and servants fill their houses. Some pull in million-dollar salaries while proclaiming Christ-likeness. They sign religious books they don't even write and sell more trinkets than the Home Shopping Network. Shame!

"The law lies paralyzed and justice wears a blindfold. Who do I pray for first? Do you really care or even hear me? Have you shut your ears?"

[Bang! Boom!]

"OK. Easy Lord. It's a bit early for a thunderstorm. You're right. I'll save the hot rhetoric later for city hall.

"Well, I can't stay on my knees all morning long, Lord. You know, prayer requires action. I'll go stand patiently and wait for your answers? Today, I'll stand down by city hall and pray outside its doors. I'll visit the mayor and the city council and warn them of impending danger. They'll look at me, again, like I'm crazy. Tonight is our mid-week prayer service at church. I'll drop by to make sure God's saints heed your call for righteousness, justice, and mercy. When I stand, please keep them from groaning, Lord.

"It's not easy being a prophet today. Give me the strength, Lord.

"Yes, I know. The righteous shall live by faith. Please help me to hold out, that I may keep the faith. Help me wait patiently for your responses to my questions!

"Amen."

BACK TO THE WORD: PROPHETIC FAITH

God told the prophet Habakkuk that "the righteous will live by his faith" (2:4). What a simple yet most powerful word from the Lord. We read this in *The Word in Life Study Bible:* "In our day, the advantage of 'living by faith' is that we can put into perspective the troubles of the world around us. Despite appearances to the contrary—when evil forces appear to have the upper hand, or when economic woes, ill health, or family circumstances appear to be doing us in—we can trust that God remains in control and that his sovereign purposes are being worked out. We know that God has said: 'The just shall live by faith.'"[1]

This profound word of faith from the Lord gave Habakkuk the strength to trust God fully and to foresee a better day ahead despite his current circumstances. "I have heard all about you, Lord, and I am filled with awe by the amazing things you have done. In this time of our deep need, begin again to help us, as you did in years gone by. Show us your power to save us. And in your anger, remember your mercy" (Hab. 3:2, NLT).

From approximately 612 to 588 BC, this Jewish prophet in the tiny land of Judah rose to speak to the people of his nation during one of the most hopeless eras in Hebrew history. Assyria was the dying world power and Babylon was the ascending giant. The prophet's homeland, Judah, soon experienced the destructive forces of the Babylonians. Habakkuk recognized the deep problems in the political, economic, moral, and religious structures of his country and its capital city, Jerusalem. His people were in the midst of a deep economic decline. Depression and destruction were on the horizon.

The prophet appealed to God, saying, "in this time of our deep need, begin again to help us." Habakkuk's understanding of the events in his day may well stimulate our faith and our churches' mission in a new decade.

Faith During In-Between Times

The prophet's request, recorded in verse 3:2, implies an interesting concept of living in an in-between time. "Lord, I have heard of your fame; I stand in awe of your deeds, O Lord. Renew them in our day, in our time make them known." Habakkuk heard about all the things that the Lord God had done for Israel in the past. He was familiar with God's deliverance of his people from slavery in Egypt under the leadership of a man named Moses. Habakkuk acknowledged God's ability to demonstrate awesome power for his chosen people in the years ahead. Just as the Jews had waited in Egypt for the future deliverer, certainly they could expect that God would deliver them again from certain calamity. Yet, in the middle of the past and the future loomed "in our time," the present age. The prophet saw his time as one of deep need for God's guidance.

Habakkuk felt that God responded too slowly to Judah's dire conditions. "How long, O Lord, must I call for your help, but you do not listen? Or cry out to you, 'violence!' but you do not save us? Why do you make me look at injustice? Why do you tolerate wrong? Destruction and violence are before me; there is strife, and conflict abounds.... justice is perverted" (1:2-3, NLT).

Habakkuk called God deaf and accused him of doing nothing to resolve Judah's woes—now. Nothing had happened to jolt his nation from a collision course with disaster. The God of heaven apparently pushed a pause button on deliverance, and Judah wallowed in an awful slump.

Is America, too, in an awful slump? Christmas shopping season 2008 was a bust, and 2009 sales fell pretty flat. Jesus refused to ante up a commercial stimulus for the economy in his name. Did our nation experience a Habakkuk-like in-between time? Do we need cleansing, healing, and recovery? Are we out of danger yet? Have we learned any lessons from the pain of the past decade? Will the church today lead our nation to moral and spiritual revival, or will it succumb to the ruins of hopelessness spreading through our land?

GO AND DO LIKEWISE

Stock market brokers and financial advisers usually caution clients to "stay in the market for the long haul." Spiritually, however, Habakkuk reminds us to stay in God's hands over the long haul. One may turn to Susie Orman, Ali Velshi, or Jim Cramer's "Mad Money," but they are also confounded and shout at one another out of frustration, fear, and anxiety.

So stay in the Lord's hands over the long haul. In the spirit of Habakkuk (2:4), be faithful and trust God fully! As Christians enduring in the church age, here are some other suggestions that will help ignite spiritual revival in our land:

1. Take ample time to pray together as people of God. Work together and serve God together. Hitch a ride to church, or

call a friend for transportation. Go to church any way you can, whenever you can, and worship together. The church is the instrument of God to bring light to a dark and sinful generation. Even if you're broke and don't have a dime for the collection plate, make your way to the cross of Christ and worship. One day, God will refill your empty pockets. Lift up prayers and holy hands together (1 Tim. 2:8).

2. Repent of personal sins and ask for healing in our churches among the people of God. Cry out to God for church unity, vision, and a missionary fervor. Remember what the Lord said to Solomon: "if my people, who are called by my name, will humble themselves and pray and seek my face and turn from their wicked ways, then I will hear from heaven and will forgive their sin and will heal their land" (2 Chron. 7:14).

3. Go into the forgotten areas of America and serve as soldiers of the cross of Christ. The church must go everywhere to rescue the perishing, lost, hurting, and hopeless people around us. As we sacrifice for the good of all, God will bless us, keep us, and provide for our needs.

4. Witness to others about God's amazing grace in the past and of God's sure mercies in the future. Show that you possess great faith in hard times like the prophet Habakkuk. Don't let anything separate you from the love of God.

5. Study the Bible together, praise God together, and sing together. These things are medicine for the soul. Sing the Lord's songs in hard times. Support one another in this new decade. Help the church really *be* the church! It must be God's redemptive army on the march for justice and mercy and righteousness in our land. The church's Savior is the hope for our people. As the apostle Paul said, "God has chosen to make known among the Gentiles the glorious riches of this mystery, which is Christ in you, the hope of glory" (Col. 1:27).

6. Pool resources so that no one falls between the cracks. Target your limited resources like a laser beam to hit relevant human needs for Christ. Weep together when necessary,

and suffer together as needed. Anything that we lose God can restore threefold, fourfold, and more.

7. Defy backsliding or faithlessness. Look for opportunities to be the people of God in a broken world. As you minster to others, your heartaches and pains will be healed. The church often grows best in times of stress, social upheaval, and national dysfunction.

8. Stay focused on the hope we claim in Jesus Christ. Avoid hateful and contentious spirits, and do not allow the roots of bitterness to gain demonic strongholds in your spirit. Invest in a church that values all people as objects of God's love.

Look at the church more than two thousand years after Christ's resurrection. Investors have increased from the original twelve to millions. Hallelujah! Stay in the Lord's hands over the long haul.

Silent Saturday

The Saturday after Jesus' crucifixion was an in-between time in Jerusalem. People talked uneasily about Friday's execution. Some wore smiles while others ached with sorrow. The tomb sat silent and the grave guarded, but, supernaturally, God had a stimulus plan in effect. It was a holy bailout. God always has a plan. This in-between day was only a precursor to the greatest miracle in the history of the world.

Indeed, America laid on the edge of a graveyard. Other nations held symposiums to discuss life after the demise of the United States. Some people threw dirt on the anticipated U.S. corpse prematurely. But God wants to work out a miracle through people of faith—the church. We have seen deliverance in the past. In the interim, know that God is faithful! And the righteous—the just—shall live by faith. The health and welfare of America hinges upon proactive churches unashamed of sharing the Good News (gospel) of Jesus Christ with all people.

Habakkuk offered up a stimulus prayer for his people: "Though the fig tree does not bud and there are no grapes on the vines, though the olive crop fails and the fields produce no food, though there are no sheep in the pen and no cattle in the stalls, yet I will rejoice in the Lord, I will be joyful in God my Savior. The Sovereign Lord is my strength; he makes my feet like the feet of a deer, he enables me to go on the heights" (3:17-19). (Read stimulus twelve for more spiritual insights from the prophet Habakkuk.)

REFLECTION/DISCUSSION

Habakkuk's stimulus prayer can direct you forward. The prayer of Habakkuk the prophet is in chapter three, and it is considered a great Old Testament theophany (a theophany is a direct appearance or manifestation of God). This appearance came to Habakkuk in his spirit. His prayer can be used by God's people to stimulate great faith today.

1. Read the short Old Testament book of Habakkuk. What are your overall impressions of the prophet?
2. If you were Habakkuk and down on your knees praying this morning, what would your prayer have included? Write it down and share it with others.
3. What did the prophet pray for in verse 3:2-3? Recall one of your tough seasons in life. How did you get through it? How did you maintain your faith?
4. In Habakkuk 3:4-7, the prophet envisions victory over the Babylonians and praises the power of God. He describes things as though they have already happened. What is one encouraging spiritual insight that you have received from God while in prayer, meditation, Bible study, or worship? How did it help you?
5. How did Habakkuk critically question God? Is it all right to do so? Why or why not?
6. What is the role of God's church in identifying sin in our nation? How do we address such sins?
7. Ultimately, God would rescue his people from their enemies. What were God's plans for Judah's enemies? What enemies has God helped you fight off and overcome? Does this reaffirm God's faithfulness to you?

8. God has plans for your life. How will you discover them? Read Habakkuk 2:1-4 and think about whether you're willing to wait faithfully and patiently for God's answers to your questions.

9. The prophet showed great faith under adverse conditions (3:17). He made a great confession of faith. As America emerges from the first decade of the 21st Century, how can a great confession of faith stimulate you and your church? Is there a confession of faith used in your church? Study it.

On large easel paper or a white writing board, write a confession of faith for the 2010s. Pray over it and seek God's wisdom. The Lord has a great spiritual stimulus plan for you. Ask God to add more specifics and to personalize your confession of faith.

Like Habakkuk, God will make your feet swift and sure like a deer running upon the high hills of adversity. Yes, God has plans for you to achieve bold new things for his Kingdom on earth (3:19).

OUTREACH MINISTRY ACTIVITY

Put a face on poverty. In Fayetteville, North Carolina, the Cape Fear Regional Bureau for Community Action, Inc., has provided non-traditional testing for HIV/AIDS and other sexually transmitted diseases among high at-risk populations. Their staff works to eliminate drugs, diabetes, and other health disparities among minorities and economically depressed people. They serve in communities that many people fear entering. Support a similar type of organization in your area that serves so courageously. Let a family, a couple, or an individual who has been served by such an organization share their story with your church group.

Nationally, Bread for the World is a collective voice of thousands of Christians urging our nation's decision makers to end hunger at home and abroad. Bread for the World members write personal letters and emails to members of Congress to change U.S. policies, programs, and conditions that allow hunger and poverty to persist. In a bipartisan way, BFW works through churches, campuses, and other organizations to engage more people in public policy advocacy. Go online to "bread.org/about-us" for more information.

PROPHETIC FAITH STIMULUS SUMMARIZED

God wants repentance. He wants an end to mindless conspicuous consumption. He wants a change of heart, values, and lifestyles for a new decade. Turn from materialism, greed, and selfishness to serving the One God who cares for all people.

Follow God's Word over the long haul. Do not let the good seed of the gospel of Jesus Christ fall on rocky ground. Let the Word be sown in fertile soil in your heart.

The resurrection proved that stock in Jesus never fails.

Look for opportunities every day to be a man or woman of God in a broken world. Team with others to be the people of God on mission doing kingdom work. As you serve others, your own wounds will be cleansed and healed.

God always has a stimulus plan just for you. Tap into it. Someone has said, "Your purpose in life is to discover your purpose in life." Talk to Jesus, for he will reveal his plans for you. Forge an intimate relationship with the Savior. God is working miracles through people of faith in this new decade.

Faith is foundational to your spiritual stimulus. Remember, "...the righteous will live by his faith" (Hab. 2:4).

STIMULUS THREE

CLOUD NINE HOPE

Those who hope in the Lord will renew their strength.
They will soar on wings like eagles; they will run and not
grow weary, they will walk and not be faint.
—Isaiah 40:31

WHAT A WAY to end the season," I exclaimed, giving my wife a bear hug in the driveway after we finally arrived home. "Who could imagine that CJ would go off like that? Wow! I still can't believe it, and on senior night against the best basketball team in the state."

Anne was so excited that she screamed coming through the front door.

"Hope the neighbors don't think I'm crazy. I just had to get that out," she chuckled, before erupting with another shout.

"Didn't he take over that game?" I boasted like any proud father. "He was unstoppable. And what about that shake-and-bake move that left Washington High's star player frozen in his tracks? What an ESPN highlight move!"

"You're crazy," Anne laughed. "But CJ's pull-up jumper and free throw did clinch the game." She sat on the family room couch, catching her breath. A die-hard basketball mom, Anne cheered at all of CJ's home basketball games while I sometimes worked late. The come-from-behind victory in our son's last high school game left us drained. The season had been tiring, a roller coaster of ups and downs.

"You guess any of those college scouts will call now?" she asked, kicking off her shoes.

"Only God knows," I said, turning on the TV set looking for the 10:00 P.M. local late night sportscast because a television crew videotaped the game. For two years, CJ received letters from about fifty Division I and II colleges. He was a hot commodity his junior season, but in recent months the letters quit coming. CJ earned all-conference honors as a senior and ranked in the top ten percent of his class academically. Sure, he suffered through a few bad games down the stretch, but was it enough to cause such a last-minute recruiting drought?

CJ impressed the coaches at North Carolina Middle University and at a smaller school in the state. The Monday after CJ's last game, the Middle University coach called and asked to come down to sign CJ to a basketball scholarship the next week. We said OK, forgetting one other option. A month earlier, I ran into a local Baptist minister at a conference. He maintained close ties to Wake Forest University, and he watched CJ play on TV several times.

"Where's your son going to college?" he asked me during a break in activities.

"Well, he really likes Wake Forest, but we don't have that kind of money. Wake offers religious studies, music, and so many things CJ likes, but it looks like N.C. Middle's the place. He really wants to play basketball, and it's a pretty good school." I had forgotten that this particular pastor formerly headed the Baptist State Convention and that he was a big Wake Forest supporter.

"Let me see what I can do. Sounds like we need a kid like him at Wake."

Two weeks later, a letter arrived from Wake Forest offering CJ an annual $15,000 academic scholarship. Anne and I discussed the Wake option once more while CJ worked his after school job at Bojangles.

"He's not going to Wake unless he can play ball," Anne said, reading the scholarship letter again. And that pretty much ended the conversation.

The next day, while driving home on her lunch break, Anne heard someone speak to her spirit. The voice said, "call the Wake Forest basketball office." So around mid-day when she arrived home, she called information and dialed the number.

"Basketball office," a male voice answered.

"Yes, my name is Anne. There's a young man you need to see. He's my son..." That evening, after work, she told me about the call.

"The coach! You really called him?" I asked. When Anne got a spell to do something, watch out! She would do anything for her kids. She and her mom once were thrown out of a little league baseball game for yelling at the umpire. In a way, I felt sorry for the Wake coaches. And to think that on the first ring the top recruiter—not a receptionist—picked up the phone. He told Anne to send a game tape, so Anne overnighted a video tape in which CJ dunked several times in a game. A 6-2, dunking point guard with great penetration moves could not go unnoticed.

The assistant coach called back the next day.

"I want you all to come up tomorrow morning and meet the head coach," he said. We were floored! CJ couldn't believe it. Meet the head coach? On Saturday we found ourselves sitting in Coach Dave Odom's office. They offered CJ a walk-on spot on the team. Within one week, his recruiting nightmare turned into a dream-come-true opportunity to play for a major college. In addition, he landed on the team during All-American Tim Duncan's senior season.

That experience taught us to always keep hope alive!

A week later, as CJ dropped raw chicken into vats of hot grease on his job, a local newspaper reporter called. Then CJ called us that night from Bojangles.

"Guess what?"

"What?" I responded.

"Brett Friedlander called from the newspaper. He interviewed me tonight."

"Whhaatt?"

"He found out that Wake Forest promised me a spot on the team. It'll be in the paper tomorrow morning." Sure enough, the next day's (May 2, 1996) lead front page sports headline in the *Fayetteville Observer* read: "Johnson On 'Cloud 9' About Joining Deacons."

BACK TO THE WORD: CLOUD NINE HOPE

"But those who hope in the Lord will renew their strength. They will soar on wings like eagles; they will run and not grow weary, they will walk and not be faint" (Isa. 40:31). Hope means favorable and confident expectation. It anticipates the fulfillment of our needs. As Christians, we must hold fast to hope during daunting challenges. After the economic, social, moral, ethical, and political upheavals of the past decade, the Beatitudes of Matthew 5:3-10 provide a treasure chest of hopeful blessings promised to Christ's disciples. They provide ample encouragement for us to stride to victory in this new decade.

The word *beatitude* means blessedness and great bliss or happiness. But Jesus' declarations of blessedness in the fifth chapter of the gospel of Matthew do not promise the generic happiness of the world. Rather, they promise a unique brand of heavenly blessedness and satisfaction to people who welcome God's gracious and indwelling presence into their lives. This Holy Presence caused Anne, CJ, and me to maintain hope despite our somewhat disappointing circumstances. The Beatitudes of Jesus tell us that we are already blessed, just as the Messiah told the poor, hungry, and thirsty crowd surrounding him centuries ago.

Jonathan Wilson-Hartgrove offered this assessment of the Beatitudes in a recent article:

> In the crowd are "people...with various diseases, those suffering severe pain, the demon-possessed, those having seizures, and the paralyzed." Jesus has in front of him everyone who, according to the religious system of his day, is cursed. Here are all the losers, anxious for Jesus to let them in on the secret. Jesus does what no religious teacher had ever done before: he calls them blessed...."You are already blessed." Jesus offers his most

important teaching to people who've failed at religion. He seems to have hope that they are the ones who will get what he is saying.[1]

As the Lord stood up to teach the multitudes, he felt a deep and abiding understanding of their weaknesses and personal needs. He stood not to criticize, but to proclaim their blessed condition, no matter what the circumstances. The Beatitudes, therefore, can stimulate hopefulness in the masses of God's people today. We all need to take time in our wearisome schedules to find hope in Jesus' declarations of our blessedness.

Blessed are the poor in spirit, for theirs is the kingdom of heaven (Matt. 5:3).

"Poor in spirit" people know they need God. In Alex Haley's epic book *Roots,* an African father named Omoro held up his newborn baby boy (Kunta Kinte) to the stars one night as part of the child's naming ritual. Looking up at the heavens with Kunta in his arms, Omoro said, "Behold—the only thing greater than yourself."[2] Indeed, blessed is the person who grows up knowing their need for God. They know that the human spirit is incomplete without the guidance of the Holy Spirit.

Some years ago, a young preacher took a pastorate at a large church and admitted to the head deacon that he did not know how to do many things. The young cleric then added, "But I know the One who does know." The inexperienced preacher was willing to be instructed by God and by God-sent people.

In the Old Testament book of Jeremiah, God told the prophet to go down to the potter's house and watch the potter making a clay vessel on a spinning wheel. Jeremiah saw the vase become flawed in the potter's hands. The potter reformed the clay and re-shaped a more perfect vase. "Poor in spirit" people realize that they are flawed and need repairs by the Divine Potter. They undergo remolding. They receive biblical instructions gladly, remain teachable by the leading of the Holy Spirit, and surrender to the Potter's hands.

Blessed are those who mourn, for they shall be comforted (Matt. 5:4).

Mourners show compassion for other people. Have you mourned someone's loss of a job, their loss of a mate through divorce, or the loss of a son or daughter to a drunk driver? There are many things people lose in life, including health, independence, freedom, and even hope. Those who show deep concern for others' hurts will receive comfort from God in their times of need.

Luke's parable of the Good Samaritan (10:27-37) tells the story of a Samaritan who mourned the injuries of a Jewish man left on the Jericho road to die. Earlier, a preacher and a deacon passed by the crime scene, lending no assistance. But the Samaritan mourned this victim of beating and robbery so much that he stopped and bandaged the man's wounds, placed him on his animal, and walked with him to an inn to let the victim rest and heal. The Samaritan mourned the condition of a man he did not know and treated him as his neighbor.

There is much to mourn in our society today. There are child and spouse abuse, miseducation of children, high incarceration rates, the working poor, abortion, illiteracy, and children in poverty wandering our streets. That is only a sampling; the list of social ills is much more extensive than that. God's people must not pass by the problems and ignore them on the road of life. Sometimes God calls us to mourn over serious conditions and be willing to act to change them.

When have you seen someone stranded beside a road with a disabled car? Did you ever take time to help while others sped onward? When have you bought a sandwich for a beggar who is hungry? If you bless others, you will be blessed. The Bible says, "Give, and it will be given to you. A good measure, pressed down, shaken together and running over, will be poured into your lap. For with the measure you use, it will be measured to you" (Luke 6:38). People need comforting, and one way to get comfort is to give it.

Blessed are the meek (gentle), for they shall inherit the earth (Matt. 5:5).

Meek or gentle people display a quiet confidence in themselves. They do not scream very much, and they do not push and shove their way through the world. They humble themselves before God and feel comfortable in their own skin. Their feelings are not easily bruised because they stay connected to life-giving Spirit, like grape branches abiding in a healthy vine. Gentle people produce good fruit because they are well connected to the True Vine, Jesus Christ.

When meek people speak up, their words carry positive impact. They speak and act from an inner voice that filters out selfishness from decision making. They can assert without aggression. They tune into station WWJD (what would Jesus do?). They stand secure among a crowd, choosing most often to respect people. Meek Christians are not wimps, but strong advocates for God, and they are not willing to let their personal agendas and whims interfere with God's will. They humble themselves before the Lord, knowing that God will exalt them.

Remember the commercial advertising E.F. Hutton? "When E.F. Hutton speaks, everybody listens." Likewise, the inner voice of the Spirit of God allows meek and gentle ones to inherit great respect and influence among their peers. This gentle approach runs counter to worldly wisdom which teaches that "the squeaky wheel gets the grease." Sometimes so much squeaking drives others away. There is a time and place for the softer approach. People will eventually recognize these gentle giants, because they inherit the respect of many contemporaries on earth.

Blessed are those who hunger and thirst for righteousness, for they shall be filled (Matt. 5:6).

Do you remember a time when you badly needed a glass of water? Maybe dehydration was about to set in. I recall priming (picking) tobacco during hot summers in North Carolina. Temperatures often climbed well above one hundred degrees between the tobacco rows, which stretched longer than a soccer field. When we came to the end of a row, our bodies desperately craved water. Thank God, a worker waited for us with a big bucket of cool water and a ladle to quench our thirst.

In a like manner we should thirst for God. We should crave what is right in the eyes of God, and earnestly seek to live out the teachings of Scripture. Be hearers and doers of God's Word, as James said (1:22). "As the deer pants for streams of living water, so my soul pants for you, O God," said the psalmist. "My soul thirsts for God, for the living God" (Ps. 42:1-2). You must greatly desire a life of integrity and honesty before the Lord.

Thirsty people of God seek righteousness. They yearn to do the right things, for the right reasons, with the right attitudes, and to the glory of God. When we free ourselves of excessive worldly cravings, we will not be blown away with every wind of society, every new gadget, every new fad, or every new style. We will be filled with God's righteousness and his blessings. We will be satisfied walking, talking, and enjoying an intimate relationship with the Holy One.

Blessed are the merciful, for they will be shown mercy (Matt. 5:7).

Mercy is love in action. It not only recognizes a need but responds to that need, even when the person in need does not merit our compassion.

At the cross of Jesus Christ we find mercy at its best. The psalmist said, "Mercy and truth have met together; righteousness and peace have kissed" (Ps. 85:10). This is the story of the cross: mercy and truth met together on our behalf. Righteousness and peace kissed each other, and heaven saw our deep need for salvation. We were drowning in sin and rebelling against the will of God. Sin left us hopeless and depressed. But at the cross, Jesus mercifully died as a substitution for our sins. He died for us, when all humanity should have hung on that cross.

What mercy! "And being found in appearance as a man, he humbled himself and became obedient to death—even death on a cross!" (Phil. 2:8). In order to save or rescue us, he took the form of a servant here on earth, leaving his glory in heaven. He allowed his flesh to be broken, and he bled for our sins.

Merciful Christians can show awesome kindness toward others. They can strive to love others as Christ loved us. It is so easy to judge and criticize people when mercy is the reaction they need most. In his moment of despair in 2009, golfer Tiger Woods needed Christians praying for his spiritual life and for his connection to God. He needed intercessors on earth lifting him up, not more critics to demean him publicly. Our society desperately needs merciful Christians acting on behalf of other people. Merciful people will receive mercy from the Lord.

Blessed are the pure in heart, for they shall see God (Matt. 5:8).

We live in such a polluted country that it is getting harder and harder to see the stars at night. Traveling in Zambia, Africa, years ago, I endured a tiring all-day automobile trip from Lusaka, the capital city, to a small town in northern Zambia. In route, my car blew out three tires on a rugged road. When I arrived at a little motel in that town late at night, the business was closed, but a stranger kindly volunteered to walk up the street and find the owner.

Sitting on my suitcase waiting, I looked up to the sky. WOW! Hundreds and hundreds of stars sparkled above my head. No. Thousands. Surely, millions! I'd never seen such a display of midnight lights back home. They seemed so clear and so close that I almost reached out to touch them. The remote Zambian sky was so free of pollutants that I saw the heavens above with new awe and praise.

The pure-in-heart person sees God as clearly as I saw those stars. He or she searches the Scriptures and takes time for daily devotions with the Lord. They regularly pull out their spiritual telescopes to delve into the heart of God, to seek the will of God. They disallow the smog of sin and evil to cloud their view of heaven. They allow the Holy Spirit of God to lift them above the haze of the world to view the very face of the Creator. From the throne room of God, they can see more of what God sees. The supernatural, omni-ocular nature of God provides the pure in heart with divine lenses to view the world and God's handiwork more clearly. From such an awesome vantage point they can slog through any wilderness on earth, because they are blessed with divine vision and clarity.

John the apostle was physically located on the isle of Patmos off the coast of Greece, but he was lifted by the Holy Spirit one Sunday to view the victory of the saints in heaven in the age to come. The Spirit of God lifted the prophet Ezekiel to see clearly the plight of the Jewish exiles who were captive in Babylon. And God gives us visions and reveals divine plans to us.

The pure in heart truly seek God avidly each day. They become transparent before the Father, confessing their sins and agreeing with God on their defects and shortcomings. They avoid acting defensively because they want to offer themselves as living sacrifices for God. As the Apostle to the Gentiles wrote, "I urge you, brothers, in view of God's mercy, to offer your bodies as living sacrifices, holy and pleasing to God—this is your spiritual act of worship" (Rom. 12:1).

When our hearts and minds are purified by the Holy Spirit, we will be blessed to see God more clearly and share our heavenly wisdom with others. We will receive hope and instill hope, and we must practice this often.

Jesus once healed a man in two stages. After the first touch of the Master, the blind man saw what he thought were walking trees—the blur of people moving around him (Mark 8:24). Then, "once more Jesus put his hands on the man's eyes. Then his eyes were opened, his sight was restored, and he saw everything clearly" (8:25). A pure heart, nurtured by the ongoing touches of the Almighty, sees more clearly.

In this story, Jesus took the blind man away from the town (away from distractions) to heal him. The pure in heart must take devotional time with God away from the distractions of our world to more clearly see God and to enjoy an intimate relationship with him.

Blessed are the peacemakers, for they will be called sons of God (Matt. 5:9).

Oh, the glory of being a peacemaker. My mother was a peacemaker and the Ralph Bunche (a great U.S. diplomat) of our family. She would not allow disharmony to reign in her home. An ambassador who quickly, but lovingly, brought warring parties to the peace table (usually her dinner table), she humbly forced us to her peace talks. She possessed a secret weapon: awesome cooking skills. Everything she touched tasted heavenly. Once lured to her table, ill tempers and bad feelings evaporated.

Peacemakers hold the peace of God within their spirits. "And the peace of God, which transcends all understanding, will guard your hearts and your minds in Christ Jesus" (Phil. 4:7). Truth and love are the recipes for peacemakers. They embody peace and skillfully pass it on to others.

Peacemakers build bridges instead of tearing them down. They are thankful that Jesus Christ built a bridge for them from earth to heaven, from sin to salvation.

Peacemakers bring people together amid the tensions of a post-recession era. The Bible says they shall be called the sons and daughters of God. They hold high positions in the kingdom of God because they help heal our land. Ask God to make you a peacemaker and peacekeeper.

Blessed are those who are persecuted because of righteousness, for theirs is the kingdom of heaven (Matt. 5:10).

Jesus said "Blessed are you when people insult you, persecute you and falsely say all kinds of evil against you because of me. Rejoice and be glad, because great is your reward in heaven, for in the same way they persecuted the prophets who were before you" (Matt. 5:11-12).

There needs to be a little prophet in us all. Prophets demand obedience to God's righteousness while they tell evil people about themselves, speaking truth to both the powerful and to the powerless. They tell kings, presidents, governors, mayors, city council representatives, and religious leaders what God demands. They take the hits of persecution and criticism because they value God's opinion more than the opinions of the rich and powerful, and more than the opinions of their friends or relatives. They fight for justice. They champion grace and love for all races, ages, creeds, colors, sexes, lifestyle orientations, and faiths. Prophets also warn of the wrath of God for those who transgress his laws.

They may get persecuted in the world, but the blessing of an eternal heavenly home is promised to them. "Anyone who receives a prophet because he is a prophet will receive a prophet's reward, and anyone who receives a righteous man because he is a righteous man will receive a righteous man's reward" (Matt. 10:41).

GO AND DO LIKEWISE

Hope is not naive. It does not say that all problems will cease. Hope does not promise a life void of storms and troubles. Hope is familiar with the gravity of problems around us. And yet, hope is ever present to carry us through the storms. David went through the valley of the shadow of death, and he feared no evil (Ps. 23). The God of hope traveled with him through the valley and helped him emerge in the light of a better day. This is the promise of hope in this new decade, that knowing Good News and mercy follow us even in times of trouble.

"But those who hope in the Lord will renew their strength. They will soar on wings like eagles; they will run and not grow weary, they will walk and not be faint" (Isa. 40:31). There will be days when living in a challenging new decade will weary and tire us. Even so, God's great strength is never diminished. When life comes at us fast with a mound of problems, we must call on Almighty God just as fast.

In Hebrew, the phrase "wait upon" means to expect, to look for patiently, to hope, and to be confident in God. "Wait upon" is a verb meaning to bind together or gather together. Our challenge is to always gather together hope. Hope is a great theme of the Bible from cover to cover. It is alive even when it appears crucified. Jesus confidently said, "Father, into thy hands I commend my spirit." Hope never dies. We should never allow Satan to convince us there is no hope left. Many have perished because they lost all hope when relief loomed just minutes away. Losing hope is the Devil's trick, so we must always keep hope alive.

My brothers and sisters, "stand firm. Let nothing move you. Always give yourselves fully to the work of the Lord, because you know that your labor in the Lord is not in vain. But thanks be to God! He gives us the victory through our Lord Jesus Christ" (1 Cor. 15:58, 57).

In the wake of Hurricane Katrina's devastation along the Gulf Coast, our church made a donation, as did many other congregations all across America. But we wanted to do more. After six months of saving nickels, dimes, and quarters in jars, about two hundred members collected $25,000 in change. In 2007 a bus load of our youth took that offering to the Lott Carey Foreign Mission Convention in New Orleans, and the money was used to help run Hope and Resurrection Centers in that area. Our hope, coupled with that of other churches, brought hope to thousands in the midst of what seemed like hopelessness.

The Beatitudes provide hopeful promises of the blessings that come from living as faithful Christians.

REFLECTION/DISCUSSION

1. What two or three things do you hope for most in life?
2. Most people know somebody who has inspired them to hope in times of stress. What person has sparked hope for you? How did they do this?
3. Read Psalm 43, focusing on verses three to five. This is a prayer in a time of trouble. What role does prayer play in your hope for the future?
4. Look in the New Testament at 1 Peter 1:3-9, and list some of the benefits of a Christian's heavenly inheritance. Does this give you any hope?
5. How is hope an anchor of your soul (Heb. 6:19)?
6. Let these Scriptures assure you of your hope in Jesus Christ: Hebrews 11:1; Romans 8:4; Psalm 27; Psalm 146:5-9; and Isaiah 41:10.
7. Jesus tells us that disciples who live out the Beatitudes are salt and light in the world. What Beatitude means the most to you? Does one stand out? Why?

OUTREACH MINISTRY ACTIVITY

Roll up your sleeves and offer a local school assistance that gives students, teachers, parents, and administrators hope. Paint or spruce up the facilities, plant flowers, tutor children, volunteer for field trips, contribute funds for unmet needs, and pray regularly for that school. Let Christ use you and your church to instill fresh hope there.

CLOUD NINE HOPE STIMULUS SUMMARIZED

Hope means favorable and confident expectation. The Beatitudes are fertile soil for growing hope in a new decade.

Poor-in-spirit people know they need God. They are willing to change, according to the divine Teacher's instructions. They're open to change.

Blessed mourners show compassion for others, and when they bless others, they are blessed with compassion.

Meek people display confidence in who they are because they know who their Creator is. They inherit great respect and influence among their peers.

Those who hunger and thirst after righteousness do the right things, for the right reasons, with the right attitude, to glorify God. They will be filled with the fruit of good works for the kingdom of God and with great satisfaction in life.

Mercy is love in action that recognizes and responds to needs. Merciful people of God are recipients of mercy from the Lord.

The pure in heart are transformed into the salt and light of the world because they clearly see the heart of God.

Peacemakers hold high positions in the kingdom of God because they help heal our land and unite our people in hope. They are the sons and daughters of God.

S T I M U L U S   F O U R

R A D I C A L   L O V E

Love suffers long and is kind.
—1 Corinthians 13:4

G OD HIT ME with a wake-up slap in the face early one morning
while I read 1 Corinthians chapter thirteen. For the past half
decade one of my close relatives—Mack—has been addicted to the
stimulant methamphetamine (meth), a hideous drug that overtook
him like unchecked cancer. Mack possesses so many extraordinary
gifts, yet he allowed this drug to invade him like a legion of devils.
He struggles and harms himself while caught in its mind-altering
web.

Meth pushes Mack farther and farther from God and plunges
him headlong into other vices of the world. He wanders among the
living dead of society and falls deeper into despair. In the process,
he loses traction with Christ Jesus his Savior. Maybe we have all
lost some traction with our Savior at various points in our lives,
but it is in those tough times that we must guard against losing
traction with our Creator. As Moses said, "If you do what is right,
will you not be accepted? But if you do not do what is right, sin
is crouching at your door; it desires to have you, but you must
master it" (Gen. 4:7).

In the midst of my crisis with Mack, I appreciated the apostle Paul's powerful description of love found in 1 Corinthians 13:4-8. Indeed, Paul's words slapped me to my senses saying that love suffers long. It always perseveres. All other things will pass away, including prophecies, tongues (spiritual languages), and knowledge; but faith, hope, and love will never pass away. This Scripture was my wake-up call! Here God spoke to me about a radical Christ-centered love defying worldly wisdom or understanding. It is an extreme heavenly type of love that only flows forth freely from the very heart of God.

For several years my wife and I encouraged Mack, sometimes in person but more often via telephone conversations to his latest rehab site. After hours upon hours of painful talks, debates, and arguments, I suddenly shut down. I grew weary of his backsliding patterns. My love wore down to an all-time low, and I did not care to talk to him anymore.

Deep down I never quit loving Mack, or even praying for him, but I quit communicating with him. While he needed me more than ever, I needed a supernatural ability to press on, an ability that just evaded me. The agony of his predicament caused me so much pain, adversely affecting my wife and our health. My wife Anne became one of Mack's last tethers to sanity until God convicted and called me to suffer long.

Understanding the idea of love suffering long got me back in the game. Paul's dramatic depiction of love spoke to my dilemma. The same love shown to dastardly Saul (the apostle Paul's pre-Christian name) was available to me here in the 21st Century.

A Reset Button

Then one day Mack called my wife's cell phone. Anne was talking to someone else on our house phone, so she asked me to take the call.

"Hi, what's up?" I asked Mack, quickly sensing his disappointment when he heard my voice.

"Well, I know you'll tell me nothing I say makes sense," he sighed. "So please don't jump all over me this time."

"How are you doing?" I replied, all the time praying for meaningful words.

"I think I'm going back to Memphis. I can get more help there." Mack's stint in a Georgia halfway house had lasted nearly a year, but he missed his friends and relatives back home. For the next twenty minutes he talked and I listened patiently (for a change). Finally he asked, "How do you know God's will? What should I do?"

"Well, God can answer you one of three ways: Yes, No, or Wait," I said. "You have some good ideas, but your plan is still a little fuzzy. You don't seem confident about your next steps. Maybe God is saying wait until his plans for you become clearer. You can call me again and run your thoughts past me if you like."

After we prayed together over the phone, Mack thanked me for my guidance and apparently appreciated my new attitude. I knew God's radical love pushed the "reset button" in my heart. It was like the red reset button on my garbage disposal that I press when it gets clogged. At that moment, I felt my heart's reset button get pushed by divine supernatural love. All my judgmental garbage went down the drain. Except for the grace of God, I could have experienced a similar fate to Mack during my backsliding years in college. God helped me reach out to him.

Dealing with Legion

Stepping onto dry land after a tumultuous boat ride across the Sea of Galilee, Jesus immediately confronted a man full of evil spirits. The man howled like a wolf as he darted out of the tombs in the wilderness of Gadara. Numerous evil spirits possessed him. Every day he cut himself and cursed in the cemetery. People tried to bind him, but he always broke the chains and smashed the shackles.

Now when he saw Jesus, the wild man ran to worship him, which caused the evil spirits to be afraid. They knew Jesus when they heard him say, "Come out of this man, you evil spirit!" Then Jesus asked, "What is your name?" (Mark 5:8-9).

"My name is Legion; for we are many," the evil spirits responded before begging Jesus not to send them scattered abroad in the land.

So Jesus sent them into a large herd of pigs that were feeding on a nearby hillside, and the swine ran crazily into the lake and drowned.

Perhaps you know a friend, neighbor, or relative who is overwhelmed by evil and who lacks self-control. The evil forces of the world threaten to dislocate their spirit from the very image of God. This happens when evil spirits take over one's heart and mind.

Legion inside Jesus' Camp

Even as Jesus and his entourage set foot in the country of the Gadarenes, a traitor stood amidst the disciples. The gospel according to Luke tells us, "Then Satan entered Judas, called Iscariot, one of the Twelve. And Judas went to the chief priests and the officers of the temple guard and discussed with them how he might betray Jesus" (22:3-4). Yes, one of the Twelve disciples with Jesus at Gadara would eventually conspire to crucify the Lord.

How has evil influenced your life? What is your evil spirit? Could it be feelings of inferiority or superiority, selfishness, infidelity, jealousy, or drug addiction? Evil spirits destroy many lives. In the span of a month last year, the governor of South Carolina admitted his marital infidelity. Pop star Michael Jackson died of apparent misuse of prescription drugs. And football star Steve McNair—a married man—allegedly died from gunshots to the head in an apartment with his alleged girlfriend. What evil spirits threaten your life? Alcoholism, materialism, gluttony, pride, rebellion, or pornography? The traditional seven deadly sins are pride, covetousness, lust, envy, gluttony, anger, and sloth. These evils can pop up any time, like a computer virus, and they can eventually overwhelm one's system.

Israel's King David prayed to be cleansed of the evil spirit that caused him to take a man's life and then marry his wife. David cried out to God: "Have mercy on me, O God, according to your unfailing love; according to your great compassion blot out my transgressions. Wash away all my iniquity and cleanse me from my sin.... Cleanse me with hyssop, and I will be clean; wash me, and I will be whiter than snow.... Create in me a pure heart, O God, and renew a steadfast spirit within me.... Restore to me the joy of your salvation and grant me a willing spirit, to sustain me" (Ps. 51:1, 2, 7, 10, 12). King David knew the power and scope of God's great love for his people, and God cleansed and restored his servant.

Let us allow Christ to cleanse us of evil influences that separate us from the love of God. James tells us to "Submit yourselves to God. Resist the devil, and he will flee from you. Come near to God and he will come near to you. Wash your hands, you sinners, and purify your hearts, you double-minded" (James 4:7-8). And Paul assures us that "we are more than conquerors through him who loved us" (Rom. 8:37).

So many unclean things enter into us through television shows, R and X rated movies and videos, and through sexually explicit and pornographic materials found on the Internet. Evil spirits pop up from computers, cell phones, I-pods, text messages, web and Facebook pages, and twitters. They often pop up hitching a ride on a friend, relative, or co-worker who becomes close to us or who walks through our front door. Drugs and alcohol serve as incubators for evil thoughts and deeds.

Total Rehab

Jesus not only cleansed the demon-possessed man of his evil spirits, but he restored him to health. When the town came out to see what had happened, the man was sitting and clothed and in his right mind. He experienced total rehabilitation at Jesus' hands.

In addition to cleansing and restoration, Jesus went a necessary step farther. He instructed the man to go home and tell his family and his friends what the Lord has done. The man obeyed and "went away and began to tell in the Decapolis how much Jesus had done for him. And all the people were amazed" (Mark 5:20). After the Lord transformed this man's life, he became an early evangelist of the saving Good News of Jesus Christ.

The Bible urges us not to be conformed to the pattern of this world, but to "be transformed by the renewing of your mind. Then you will be able to test and approve what God's will is—his good, pleasing and perfect will" (Rom. 12:2). God's radical love and God's radical love alone has the power to cleanse, restore, and transform us to do good works. Without transformation sinners may return to old, evil habits. As a friend of mine put it, "the past wants you back." The sinful ways of yesterday are just a step away.

BACK TO THE WORD: RADICAL LOVE

The apostle Paul experienced a wake-up call in his life. He went from being church enemy number one to being a highly esteemed preacher and teacher of the Christian faith. In between these positions, Paul was blinded by a flash of light and knocked down into the dirt of Palestine's Damascus Road. There God transformed Paul with a clear vision of radical divine love (Acts chapter nine).

Today, a clear vision of God's radical love through Jesus Christ is necessary for surviving and thriving in tough times loaded with evildoers. Even Paul's name was changed from Saul. His 180-degree turnaround, from opposition to Christ to a pro-Jesus stance, was so dramatic that leaders of the early church doubted his sincerity. They feared Paul, thinking that maybe his change of heart was another trick to infiltrate the church hierarchy and bring fledgling believers to their knees.

But Paul's transformation was real. Jesus Christ spoke to Paul personally and gave him specific understanding of radical divine love. Only God's radical love principles changed Paul's hostility to, persecution of, and violence toward the church. He obeyed Christ's calling upon his life and became one of the faith's greatest evangelists. Indeed, he became the man God used to open up the gospel to the Gentiles. Jesus Christ pressed a big reset button on Paul's heart, making him the right man to tell us about this radical love of God.

The word *radical* indicates a markedly significant departure from normal human actions. Radical means extreme. Radical actions may be prompted by extreme good or by extreme evil. The underwear and shoe bombers who tried to blow up civilian airplanes could be called radicals in the worst sense by many people. Radicals put forth radical opinions and principles.

God's love, however, is radically and extremely good because it can take us to the origin of love as found in the heart of our Creator, thereby reforming our opinions and causing us to live as more perfectly loving people. In many instances today, divinely inspired loving actions are vast departures from the norm. When a parent forgives a drunk driver who killed their child, that radical love springs from heaven's wellspring of supernatural forgiveness!

God's love can be supernaturally imbedded within an individual like Paul or like any person reading this book. This love empowers believers to achieve great feats, and equips them to defy natural reason and logic. This love cleanses, restores, and transforms Christ's followers.

We Christians are called to a radical love that sometimes elicits the world's anger. The fact that God sent his Son to die for ungodly humanity is radical. "God demonstrates his own love for us in this: While we were still sinners, Christ died for us" (Rom. 5:8).

The following radical love principles were written by the apostle Paul to help us prosper and live in community with one another.

Love suffers long (1 Cor. 13:4).

Patient love helps us wait for others to go through their circumstances and emerge as better persons. We suffer with them (longsuffering) and do not cut them off from our love. Many times, we must suffer long with ourselves. We patiently wait for our spiritual maturity to develop and for us to emerge from our godless ways as better persons. Various circumstances demand tough love, which is another term for radical love. Mack needed my tough, genuine, long-lasting, and unconditional love.

Love is kind.

We must show mercy even when people reject us. Our model in this regard is God. How often has God been kind to us, even when we have been unkind to others and messed up big time? We must not quickly rebuff people because they respond negatively to us. When others respond to us in a negative way, that is an excellent time to really get their attention with our kindness. Kind love heaps burning coals on the heads of one's enemies and may bring about their repentance (Rom. 12:20; Prov. 25:21-22). Kindness is the key to godly love. Read more about godly kindness in stimulus nine.

Love does not parade itself or become boastful and proud.

Love does not drop (celebrity) names or seek to be recognized and elevated above others. It does not strut around like a proud peacock. It does not seek the praise of people for every good deed done, and it is not puffed. People hate a one-man parade! "Do not think of yourself more highly than you ought, but rather think of yourself with sober judgment, in accordance with the measure of faith God has given you" (Rom. 12:3). If you want to soberly measure your importance, just stick your fist in a bucket of water and pull it out. The hole that remains may be how much you will be missed.

Love does not behave rudely, but is courteous (13:5).

Rudeness indicates an ego that is out of control or an attitude that has run amuck. Love serves instead of embarrassing others. It is not easily provoked or easily irritated. It is not touchy, and it is not highly sensitive to unkind people. Love knows its source is in God, and is not diminished by the callousness of others.

Radical love does not think evil.

Love keeps no record of wrongs. It finds no joy in others' faults, nor does it participate in idle gossip and slander. This brand of love speaks the truth, and builds up and strengthens other people. It forgives and even forgets. It is more than fair and just; it is merciful. My dad would tell his congregation that the best way to build up your church and see it grow is by speaking well of it to other people. Church gossip is very destructive. Beware of evil criticism that negates God's love and stunts spiritual growth.

Love bears all things (13:7).

When we say that love bears all things, it means that love never gives up. It believes all things are possible and never loses faith. It hopes all things, envisions better days, and endures all things by persevering through all circumstances. Supernatural, radical love is willing and ready to trust someone and give second and third chances. Love goes the second mile and beyond, and is friends with the Good Samaritan. It never regards anyone as hopeless.

The Blemish

James W. Crawford wrote of a story about a woman with a terrible blemish. She fell in love with a blind man and married him. One day her husband found a surgeon who could give him his sight. His wife was terrified. The blind man sensed that she did not share his joy. His wife feared losing his love when he saw her blemish. The blind man loved his wife so much that he never underwent surgery. Her happiness meant more to him than his sight.[2]

Love can sacrifice like that. It can go through hell and high water, through rebellious children, abusive parents, sickness and death, economic and financial distress, home foreclosures, job losses, heartaches and pains, tragedies and misfortunes, homelessness and hunger, ups and downs, war and killings, the good, the bad, and the ugly. We can still find strength to love people while we struggle through our problems.

The apostle Paul said, "Who shall separate us from the love of Christ? Shall trouble or hardship or persecution or famine or nakedness or danger or sword?...No in all these things we are more than conquerors through him who loved us" (Rom. 8:35, 37). Also, Paul says that nothing "will be able to separate us from the love of God that is in Christ Jesus our Lord" (Rom. 8:39).

We all bear the blemishes of sin, but we must remember that "God demonstrates his own love for us in this: While we were still sinners, Christ died for us" (Rom. 5:8).

Love never fails (13:8).

Love never fails because it is never used up. It keeps on coming. The more you give radical love, the more you get. The more you throw it out, the more it sticks to somebody else and comes back to bless you. Let us not allow post-recession blues to thwart our enthusiasm to love. The radical love of God never experiences recession or depression, and it will never cease. Jesus said, "Love the Lord your God with all your heart and with all your soul and with all your strength and with all your mind and, 'Love your neighbor as yourself'" (Luke 10:27).

What has the world told you to quit? Who have you been told to give up on? If God gave radical love to Paul, then nothing is impossible to us. Terrorists may come; but love never ends. Wars will arise, but love never ends. Wall Street corporations will let us down, but love never ends. National and world leaders and governments will disappoint us, but love never fails.

The Bubbles Will Bring You Up

As an undergraduate student at the University of North Carolina—Chapel Hill in 1968, I had to pass a swimming test to graduate. Every student at UNC was expected to swim four laps of an Olympic-sized pool using three different swimming strokes. After mastering that, I was told to climb up on the *high* platform board that stood aloft near the ceiling of the swimming complex. Afraid of great heights, I listened to my instructor who said, "don't worry, the bubbles will bring you back up." I could not let one dive block my graduation, so I took the long climb up, dove in nearly touching the bottom of the pool, and I felt the mass of bubbles from my splash lifting me to the surface of the water.

Love is like those bubbles; it never fails. When you are down and appear to be drowning in a pool of troubles and despair, God's love bubbles will lift you up again! James Rowe wrote a hymn years ago affirming this principle: "Love lifted me, love lifted me, when nothing else could help, love lifted me."

46

Satan and evil are ever present, but "greater is he [Jesus Christ] that is in you, than he that is in the world" (1 John 4:4, KJV). Indeed, as Paul said, "I can do everything through him who gives me strength" (Phil. 4:13). Love is powerful. It can take the dirtiest, flea-bitten dog out of the deepest drainage ditch and use it like a prize Labrador retriever to point souls to Christ.

In times like these, Americans must tap into the deep well of God's love. That love is brighter than any sunrise, wider than any horizon at sea, and deeper than the Grand Canyon. God's love does not wear thin. It is not momentary, not short-lived, and not selfish. Radical love emerges out of the cross of Jesus Christ. It arose from Christ's long suffering; from the blood he shed on the old rugged cross. Radical love overcame the torture of the cross, the beatings of enemies, the ridicule of religious and Roman leaders, and the doubts and fears of angry crowds. How great a love that caused God to give Jesus over to death on a cross as a sacrifice for our sins. The Messiah's resurrection solidly validates the power of God's great love for us.

We will never plumb the depths of such divine love, but we must strive to plunge in deeper. We must not merely wade in God's radical love, but we need to dive headlong! We need to plunge in and swim in its depths. Mack's condition is a daily reminder to me to love him just as Christ loves me.

It is my desire to bathe in this reservoir of radical love that never runs dry. It can sustain me and my family, and you and your family, through tough times. There is no greater love, and there is no greater power.

William Cowper (1731-1800) wrote this hymn:

There is a fountain filled with blood, drawn from
Emanuel's veins,
And sinners plunged beneath that flood,
lose all their guilty stains...

The dying thief rejoiced to see that fountain in his day;
And there may I, though vile as he, wash all my sins away...

E'er since, by faith, I saw the stream thy flowing
wounds supply,
Redeeming love has been my theme, and shall be till I die:...
And shall be till I die.[3]

"And now these three remain: faith, hope and love. But the greatest of these is love" (1 Cor. 13:13).

Go and Do Likewise

Our challenge is to let God use our experiences, our struggles, heartaches, and troubles to help hurting people all around us struggling to survive. We are losing a big chunk of our young generation to illegal drugs, drive-by shootings and other types of violence, gang warfare, suicides, car accidents, and other destructive forces.

A few decades ago, a promising young basketball star named Len Bias was the second player drafted in the first round by the National Basketball Association's Boston Celtics. That same summer, he died from a drug overdose, never playing a single professional game in the NBA. His family was devastated, yet, his mom turned her grief into positive action. She became a spokesperson against drugs by urging youth to "say no!"

Allow God to help us turn our struggles and tragedies into a powerful ministry. We may have to stretch outside the comfort zone, but radical love demands it.

Reflection/Discussion

1. Have you ever felt like the demoniac in the fifth chapter of Mark, whereby you desperately needed God's help to overcome your personal evil?

2. Have you tried to help someone else whose life had spiraled out of control? What happened?

3. Which one of the "Love" phrases of 1 Corinthians 13:5-8 speaks most directly to your life situation? Why? How will you apply it to restore and transform your life?

4. Read Romans 8:31-39. The apostle asks, "Who shall separate us from the love of God?" Have you ever felt separated from God's love? When and how? How did you get reconnected? How does this Romans passage help you?

5. Paul's description of love challenges us to love people who aren't so loveable. Are you guilty of loving only those who will first love you? Is your love radical enough to love your enemies or those you dislike?

6. William Shakespeare said, "Love sought is good, but given unsought is better" (*Twelfth Night*, Act iii, scene 1). What might he have meant by that?

7. Some people have trouble showing love for other races, ethnic groups, prison inmates, ex-convicts, prostitutes, beggars, the mentally ill, and homeless and poor people. Should we love them? What other people are difficult to love?

Jesus said, "A new command I give you: Love one another. As I have loved you, so you must love one another. By this all men will know that you are my disciples, if you love one another" (John 13:34-35). What is the point our Lord is driving home?

OUTREACH MINISTRY ACTIVITY

Invite patients from a local drug rehabilitation house to your church/ministry for dinner, or take a meal to them. Let them share their stories with your group. Consider involving your youth. Lead a devotional session, pray together, and discover their needs. Offer to provide personal items to the residents for a year, or show your love by making some other tangible contribution. Offer your place of worship as a sanctuary for them to encounter God's radical love.

Consider giving support to an organization like the Salvation Army that aids many people who have lost their way in life. Their Christmas toy drives, food drives, volunteer bell ringers, and shelters aid the neediest of our neighbors. There is probably a local Salvation Army center near you.

Radical Love's Stimulus Summarized

Only Jesus Christ, the Son of God, can bind the strong man (Satan) and restore a healthy image of God within a person.

The power of God's love cleanses us from evil, restores our sanity, and transforms us to do good works under any circumstances.

Let God help you turn your difficult circumstance into a powerful ministry to people in need. Stretch outside your comfort zone because God's radical love demands it.

God's radical love can be supernaturally imbedded within you and empower you for good works.

PART TWO
INSIDER INFORMATION

YOUR HOLY DNA

But we have this treasure in jars of clay to show that this
all-surpassing power is from God.
—2 Corinthians 4:7

I WAS A shy lad with a mischievous twinkle in my eye, although
one of my sisters called the twinkle devilish. Most folks saw me as
a pretty good boy. The mothers of our church (older mature women)
often told me, "You're going to be a preacher just like your father.

"How many pieces of chicken did you eat last Sunday?" they
would inquire, as if that information foretold my future. Where
I came from, Southern fried chicken was the gourmet specialty
served to preachers most Sunday afternoons. The preacher, who
often dined at a church member's home, received first dibs on the
prime pieces of chicken—the breasts. The mothers of our church
knew that I wasn't ready to fill dad's shoes because I still took a
liking to drumsticks and thighs.

At six years old, this somewhat shy preacher's kid took a step
of faith to Jesus during a worship service in 1955 at the Martin
Street Baptist Church in Raleigh, North Carolina. The sanctuary
was jammed with more than five hundred people praising God,

and the choir was in top form while my dad preached a wise and powerful message. The day proved to be extra special.

On this particular Sunday I rose from my seat, stepped out of my pew, and walked the aisle of our church toward the altar. I stepped forward like a butterfly floating over a summer field. I offered no resistance to the force pulling me forward. I walked on my own, but I was not alone.

Oddly, the feeling reminded me of an accident I suffered a year earlier. Playing in the yard of the church parsonage, I stepped on a shovel. It gashed my leg and left me bleeding profusely. As folks ran to assist and rush me to the hospital, I told them quite calmly: "I'll be OK, God is with me."

In church that Sunday morning, I knew God was with me during this defining moment in my life. Supposedly shy and reserved, I nevertheless calmly walked forward putting my hand in my dad's hand and told him how much "I love Jesus and want to follow him." I didn't know a lot about becoming a Christian, so I certainly walked by faith that day. The old folks said, "Something's got a hold of him."

Little did I realize that God knew me in my mother's womb and already formed a plan for my life. While free to choose my destiny, I now know a holy DNA guides me through life. In science, DNA represents deoxyribonucleic acid, which is a carrier of human genetic information. This genetic information is coded into everyone differently. No DNA in any two persons is exactly the same.

Your Holy DNA

There is a holy DNA, a spiritual strain given by God running within us and carrying spiritual information about every believer. This spiritual coding is unique for each person and we must choose to tap into this resource.

Physical DNA determines certain physical traits like eye color, hair texture, height, and many other things. Holy DNA, however, is an earthly way of describing how God has blessed us with special spiritual characteristics etched inside us from birth. These spiritual characteristics include compassion, leadership, discernment, generosity, humor, diplomacy, and the like. An example would be the Old Testament warrior Samson, who received a special assignment from birth "to be a Nazirite, set apart to God from birth, and he will begin the deliverance of Israel from the hands of the Philistines" (Judg. 13:5). His great strength rescued Israel from their enemy, and all of this was foreseen while he was in the womb.

According to the Bible, the apostle Paul was ordained at Antioch by prophets in that church for his first missionary journey (Acts 13:1-4). Paul wrote in his letter to the church at Galatia, however, that God's Spirit ordained him in his mother's womb. "When God, who set me apart from birth (the womb) and called me by his grace, was pleased to reveal his Son in me so that I might preach him among the Gentiles, I did not consult any man"(Gal.1:15-16).

Likewise, Mary, the mother of Jesus, was apprised of her child's purpose even before she carried him in her womb. An angel of the Lord spoke to her, saying, "Mary, you have found favor with God. You will be with child and give birth to a son, and you are to give him the name Jesus. He will be great and will be called the Son of the Most High...his kingdom will never end" (Lk. 1:30-33).

Some natural and spiritual characteristics are set at conception, and others develop after birth. My elder son has a special, God-given ability to connect with children. He once took a pitiful YMCA basketball team of thirteen-year olds from the bottom of their league to being champions in a one-year span. He knew how to instill confidence and teamwork in those teens. His love for children and youth has always been evident.

We can use our birth blessings or we can ignore them; we can choose to use these blessings from birth to help those around us, or keep our treasures hidden and bottled up.

There was a man who traveled to a far country. Before leaving, he called his three servants and entrusted money to them. He gave one servant five bags of money, another two bags, and the other received one bag. The first two traded and invested their master's money wisely, earning good returns. The last one, who received only one bag of money, became upset with his smaller portion and denounced his master. He hid the money in the ground.

When the master returned home, the servants reported what they did with his money. The servants with five and two bags had doubled the master's money and were praised, but the servant who received one bag said, "Sir, I know you are a hard man, harvesting crops you didn't plant and gathering crops you didn't cultivate. I was afraid I would lose your money, so I hid it in the earth and here it is" (Matt. 25:24-25, NLT).

The master replied, "You wicked and lazy servant! You should at least have put my money into the bank so I could have some interest." The master took his bag of money and gave it to another servant. The gifts and talents given to us must be used wisely. We are born with some abilities, but they must be cultivated and used for the betterment of humanity. Other abilities are bestowed upon us during the course of our lives, and they also need similar wisdom. When we receive Christ Jesus as our Lord and Savior, God gives each Christian a gift or gifts (special abilities) to help the church prosper in its work. We must put our gifts to good use and never hide them.

Bees And Bugs

My dad once told me that scientists claimed the bumblebee's body is too heavy for its small wings and should not be able to fly. Fortunately, dad said, the bumblebee knew nothing about the scientific claims and just kept on flying. He said the lightning bug (firefly), when dissected to determine what makes it light up, is simply full of mushy stuff. Therefore, God has given us abilities and we need to soar with them, no matter what others may say we cannot do. Like the lightning bug, God has given us the right stuff to perform special good works and light up our world.

The bags of money in the Bible parable are symbols of God's many resources given to men and women. Like the bee and the lightning bug, we must use our God-given abilities, those things etched in our holy DNA, for the glory of God. We must not be jealous of other believers' gifts and talents, but we must use what is in our hands! What valuable stuff has God entrusted to you?

Spiritual abilities are special to a person, but there are some spiritual traits and abilities that may be part of a common strain among family members. The apostle Paul pointed out to Timothy that his family members were blessed with a strain of great faith: "I have been reminded of your sincere faith, which first lived in your grandmother Lois and in your mother Eunice and, I am persuaded, now lives in you also. For this reason I remind you to fan into flames the gift of God, which is in you through the laying on of my hands. For God did not give us a spirit of timidity, but a spirit of power, of love and of self-discipline" (2 Tim. 1:5-7).

No two people will use similar traits exactly the same way. We must pay particular attention to stir up our gifts in order to accomplish the special purpose God wants to achieve through us.

A Holy DNA Flashback

Just after the turn of the 20th Century, a Baptist pastor named Lee Henderson Johnson of Oxford, North Carolina, took Ida Faison, a public school teacher, for his wife. To this union Paul Harold Johnson was born on June 22, 1913. As a youngster, Paul enjoyed following his father to his churches on Sundays. As Paul grew older, he drove his father's Model-T Ford, chauffeuring his dad to the four churches he served. As a teen, he sometimes ended up at church programs when he would rather be playing with the boys in Oxford.

During his grammar school years, Paul encountered difficulties reading. Some people thought he was a slow learner, but one day a new teacher, Mrs. Moon, came to his school. She took special interest in Paul and soon discovered that the root of his problem was poor eyesight. Paul was fitted with glasses and his grades soared. A sincere concern for people was already mixed in his holy DNA and Mrs. Moon further ignited Paul's compassionate heart.

Young Paul could have been a great businessman. He was organized, disciplined, thrifty, and ingenious. But a pastor's heart of awesome compassion for people was stamped upon him in his mother's womb. It was nurtured by a fatherly and motherly image in the home, and by a loving teacher in the classroom.

The psalmist says, "For you created my inmost being; you knit me together in my mother's womb. I praise you because I am fearfully and wonderfully made; your works are wonderful, I know that full well. My frame was not hidden from you when I was made in the secret place. When I was woven together in the depths of the earth, your eyes saw my unformed body. All the days ordained for me were written in your book before one of them came to be" (Ps. 139:13-16).

Later in life, Paul Johnson felt a call to preach, much like his dad felt many years earlier. The holy DNA preaching strain ran in the family as his dad and an older brother were preachers. People in Oxford predicted the same would happen to Paul. Very often the sign of a calling to preach is preceded by the faith community's awareness of the gift, even before the gift's recipient knows.

"As a boy, I would preach funerals for dogs and cats in the neighborhood," Rev. Johnson recalled years later. "Everybody would bring their pets to me. As I got older, I went out into the woods to preach to the trees. I don't really know whether I thought I was preaching to the trees, but I was going to a quiet place where I could preach and wouldn't be heard."

Paul Harold Johnson was my father. When he shared the story about his preaching at pet funerals, I saw a similar pattern in my life. I remember, as a boy, sneaking into my dad's church on Saturdays when nobody was around. Our church had an outdoor chime system that played Christian music on Sunday mornings to the surrounding community. One Saturday, I cut on the sanctuary microphone system and acted like I was preaching to a crowd in that empty church. I could picture the pews being filled, so I preached with all my might. Little did I realize that the microphone system was somehow hooked into the outside speaker system. People all over our neighborhood heard me preaching, but not a soul told me until years later.

My father was licensed by the First Baptist Church in Oxford in 1934, and he went on to complete his bachelor and master of divinity degrees at Shaw University in Raleigh. Later on he received the doctor of divinity degree from the same school. His daughter

Delcie became a deacon of a church just outside Denver, Colorado, and his younger daughter Nita is a student at Duke Divinity School in Durham, and a postulant for holy orders of the Episcopal Diocese of North Carolina. His youngest son Cureton is the author of this book.

Dr. Johnson was once the boy who read poorly and struggled in elementary school. He went on to pastor the same church for thirty-nine years. That church included twelve hundred members. Mrs. Moon taught him this poem:

> Dare to do right, dare to be true,
> You have a task none other can do.
> Do it so kindly, so bravely, so well;
> Angels will hasten the news to tell.
>
> Dare to do right, dare to be true,
> Failings of other men will never save you.
> Stand by your conscience, your honor, your faith;
> Stand like a hero and fight until death.
>
> —author unknown

BACK TO THE WORD: YOUR HOLY DNA

Jesus once said the kingdom of heaven is like treasure hidden in a field. "When a man found it, he hid it again, and then in his joy went and sold all he had and bought that field" (Matt. 13:44). The apostle Matthew does not identify this man as a preacher, deacon, apostle or disciple. Whoever he was, this short parable teaches us about the incomparable value of the gospel for people from all walks of life. The good news of Jesus Christ will cause us to forsake frivolous things so we may possess the greatest treasure of all—faith and hope in Jesus Christ, the forgiveness of sins, and the promise of eternal life.

The apostle Paul said, "But we have this treasure in jars of clay to show that this all-surpassing power is from God and not from us" (2 Cor. 4:7). This treasure in vessels of clay is a powerful metaphor about the trust God bestows upon each disciple. We have the power of the mind of Jesus Christ and the treasures of heaven in fragile earthenware bodies. The Good News is given not primarily to the angels, but to a weak humanity subject to sickness, exhaustion, temptations, aging, and selective memory. In our toxic world, it is gifted Christians who must produce extraordinarily fruitful works that stimulate good in society.

We become better aware of our godly blessings (holy DNA) as we read Scripture.

God's Word is "a lamp to my feet and a light for my path" (Ps. 119:105). By knowing the mind of God through the Bible, we are allowed to perceive God's great plans for us. We come to know our purpose in life. Therefore, we are better prepared to recognize God's holy DNA working in and through us.

Spiritual knowledge and abilities are given to us by the Holy Spirit of God.

Jesus once told his disciples that when he, the Spirit of truth comes, "he will guide you into all truth. He will not be presenting his own ideas; he will be telling you what he has heard. He will tell you about the future. He will bring me glory by revealing to you whatever he receives from me. All that the Father has is mine; this is what I mean when I say that the Spirit will reveal to you whatever he receives from me" (John 16:13-15, NLT). Jesus still reveals his truth to us through his Spirit, defining our mission in the context of divine mission and empowering us for great works. This Spirit resource is far greater than the U.S. Library of Congress.

Imminent preacher and theologian Gardner C. Taylor has said that God stamps a DNA upon one's preaching. "Never falsify your DNA," Taylor once told preachers. "Never try to be somebody else."[1] No one of us should ever mimic another person, another Christian leader, or another disciple. We cannot be another Billy Graham, Vashti M. McKenzie, T.D. Jakes, Jim Wallis, William Augustus Jones, Mother Teresa, David E. Goatley, or Rosa Parks. We can only be ourselves. What God has given to each of us individually is for our own unique use in building the Kingdom and influencing the world for Jesus Christ.

Taylor's advice really came home to roost for me. As I prepared to preach the third night of revival at a Raleigh church, the dean of America's great preachers, Dr. Taylor himself, walked in and sat at the back of the church. At first, I thought about panicking, but a voice said, "I have prepared you to preach to anybody." God reassured me that my evening message had theological depth and spiritual fire. I just needed to stand up and proclaim what heaven sent me to tell God's people. I simply let God use my earthen vessel for the Kingdom's purpose. After the service, Dr. Taylor shook my hand with a warm smile upon his face and spoke kindly of my evening message.

A Tip from American Idol

The TV reality show *American Idol* invites many contestants from around the country to audition and hopefully win a lucrative recording contract as the best singer in the competition. The judges hear hundreds of good singers, but they often look for the voice that is not only good, but that stands out and has a certain sound unlike others in the music market.

"Even in the case of lifeless things that make sounds, such as the flute or harp, how will anyone know what tune is being played unless there is a distinction in the notes? Again, if the trumpet does not sound a clear call, who will get ready for battle?" (1 Cor. 14:7-8). God gave us special abilities that will stand out from other people. Others may do things much like we do, but they are never exactly like us. Invest your gifts in our society and make a difference for humanity!

Prayer taps you into God-given abilities for good.

One day, after being asked how to pray by his disciples, Jesus taught them the model prayer, which is recorded in Luke 11:2-4. Later, he said, "So I say to you: Ask and it will be given to you; seek and you will find; knock and the door will be opened to you. For everyone who asks receives; he who seeks finds; and to him who knocks, the door will be opened" (11:9-10). His words speak to us about the power of prayer. When we sincerely ask the Lord, for his will for our lives, our holy DNA rises like cream to the top. Prayer directs us to our special abilities and guides us in their proper use.

Our holy DNA is perfect, but we will never use it perfectly.

Adam and Eve were born in perfect fellowship with God but their perfection was marred by the world's temptations. We, too, have been given holy things by God but we carry them in imperfect vessels of clay. We will never use the holy things of God perfectly. We are instructed to "aim for perfection" (2 Cor.13:11). While we are not perfect, the Lord Jesus will "equip you with everything good for doing his will" (Hebrews 13:21).

We know that people are "born in sin and shaped in iniquity," and that we come into the world with sinful and wicked human characteristics that are not ordained by God. Still, God has the power to correct our bad traits as we surrender our lives to Jesus Christ and grow in our faith. So let us pray that God increases the good and helps us overcome the bad. Let the Master accentuate the positives and cleanse us from the negatives. Indeed, "I can do everything through him who gives me strength" (Phil. 4:13).

A SUFFERING HOLY DNA

Our ability to sacrifice and even suffer for the sake of our Christian efforts is part of our holy DNA. Jesus was born to suffer on our behalf. Likewise, we will sometimes suffer for the advancement of the kingdom of God. "For it has been granted to you on behalf of Christ not only to believe on him, but also to suffer for him" (Phil. 1:29).

The world closely observes how Christians endure suffering. If we suffer in the power of the Spirit of Christ, what a powerful testimony we become to humanity. Our long suffering reveals the loyal fruitfulness of the holy DNA God entrusted to us.

As a reporter for the *Raleigh Times* newspaper many years ago, I came to greatly respect a powerful clergy woman named Bishop E.M. Lawson. Bishop Lawson operated two shelters and ministered to the needs of drifters, homeless people, and displaced families in the inner city of Raleigh. She helped the unemployed find jobs and raised funds to help poor families with their utility bills.

On an October day in 1980, Bishop Lawson was gunned down and killed by robbers in front of the Ever-Ready Church of Christ that she founded. She paid the ultimate sacrifice for her service to the Lord, and her life has inspired me to be a cross-bearing disciple for Jesus.

We can all get better and do better in using our gifts from God. Maybe we were born in poverty or with a silver spoon in our mouths. Maybe we have endured homelessness or built magnificent subdivisions. Maybe we have been jobless or maybe we have employed scores of people. Whatever our experience, let it serve God's plans. Have you been put down, run down, or maybe even shot down? Have you shouldered heavy burdens, traveled difficult roads, seen a Golgotha (Jesus' place of crucifixion) of your own, or felt the pain of humiliation? If so, keep in mind that if anyone is in Christ, that person is a new creation; old things have passed away, and all things have become new. God can remove our vices and install his righteousness. "We are hard pressed on every side, but not crushed. Perplexed, but not in despair; persecuted, but not abandoned; struck down, but not destroyed" (2 Cor. 4:8-9). We still carry God's spiritual treasures and our holy DNA potential is magnificent.

Your Witnessing DNA

Every Christian receiving Jesus Christ by faith is encoded with a witnessing DNA. In the book of Acts, we read that "you will receive power when the Holy Spirit comes on you; and you will be my witnesses in Jerusalem, and in all Judea and Samaria, and to the ends of the earth" (1:8). We are encoded to lift up Jesus Christ before fallen humanity. The Holy Spirit of God is given to us from above upon receiving Christ by faith. Not only does the Spirit empower believers to be his witnesses, but the Spirit of God gives us special gifts and talents encoded into our holy DNA allowing us to build up the church, the people of God, and minister to others in our spheres of influence (1 Cor. 12:1-11).

Winning a million dollar lottery might be tremendous, but we do not need that to make us great and glorious. God has given all Christians the greatest treasure of all time—heaven and eternal life! This is "Christ in you, the hope of glory," in the words of Paul

(Col. 1:27). The early apostles were fishermen, tax collectors, and tent makers, yet they were entrusted to herald the Good News of salvation through faith in Jesus. They were acutely aware of their defects and weaknesses. Paul even mentioned he had a thorn in the flesh, "a messenger of Satan" that harassed him periodically. But this did not hinder him from becoming a great evangelist and our most prolific New Testament writer.

A modern example might be Pope John Paul II, who died a few years ago. He was used mightily by God to reach millions of people around the world for Christ Jesus. The pope's holy DNA was put to great use.

Go and Do Likewise

My personal relationship with God was cemented early in life when he blessed me with great interest in and strong inclination for social activism. As a youth, I marched in the civil rights demonstrations in downtown Raleigh. At an early age the Lord revealed within me social justice abilities. A few years later, I founded the African-American student newspaper, *Black Ink*, at the University of North Carolina in Chapel Hill. As a student leader, I participated in demonstrations against unfair wages and working conditions for employees on campus. I walked with Rev. Ralph Abernathy on our campus a few months after Dr. Martin Luther King, Jr. was killed. I struggled with my faith at times, but Christ always returned me to his will. The Spirit would sometimes realign my activism to conform to heaven's priorities.

Years later, I was arrested at the South African embassy in Washington, D.C., while protesting that nation's apartheid policies. Police officers locked me up with hundreds of other protestors, including Congressman John Lewis of Georgia. The social justice DNA still runs deep within me.

The Greatest Social Activist

Nevertheless, my greatest activism is to boldly lead others to faith in Jesus. More than five hundred persons accepted Christ and were baptized during my two dozen years as a pastor. Leading people to believe and receive Jesus Christ is the most liberating of all experiences. When we submit to the will of God and allow our holy DNA to be used by God, our impact on the world is multiplied exponentially. God uses us to call other people to Christian discipleship, and they are empowered to do the same. There is no greater social activism in the world!

The Jesus movement is the greatest social activist network the world has ever known. Early "believers of the Way" sparked a faith movement (spiritual stimulant) that has changed millions of lives for more than two thousand years. The apostle Paul once told his young protégé Timothy that "the things you have heard me say in the presence of many witnesses entrust to reliable men who will also be qualified to teach others" (2 Tim. 2:2).

The Creator will bless and multiply our spiritual gifts, so let God use them more fully. Pray that more of your life is surrendered to God's holy purpose. Seek the Lord and come to know the potential he placed within you. Our families, our churches, and our communities need our gifts and talents. Our rural areas, towns and cities, our nation, and the world all need a renewed and revived you.

REFLECTION/DISCUSSION

1. Have you ever felt like the hand of God was leading you in a particular direction? How?
2. Do you have a special gift from God; something you feel you were endowed with from birth? What is it and have you used it wisely?
3. Some people are gifted by God for special work but don't want to accept God's desire for their life. What would the parable of the talents in Matthew 25:14-30 suggest to you?
4. Does God know us even before birth? What does Psalm 139:13-16 suggest to you? Does God have a plan for our lives?
5. How have you discovered your holy DNA potential through Scripture reading and reflection, through prayer, and through God's Spirit touching your heart and mind? Are

there other ways to come to know your holy DNA? Does your faith community have a role to play?

6. What similar holy DNA strains seem to run in your family heritage? Is there a line of teachers/educators, carpenters, auto mechanics, inventors, or artistic folks in your family? How are they similar; how different?

OUTREACH MINISTRY ACTIVITY

Operation In-As-Much is a national ministry assisting churches in mission work in their local communities. On one designated day, a church (or several churches) undertakes multiple mission projects in their town. This could be repairing homes, taking food to shut-ins, doing health screenings, writing letters to soldiers, collecting items for a food bank, taking gifts to nursing homes, or any other project. There's something for every person to do no matter what age or ability. For one day during the year, everybody floods their city with kindness and good works. Get involved in your community in this way by contacting the national Operation In-As-Much office at 4815 Santa Monica Road, Knoxville, Tennessee, 37918. The telephone number is 865-765-1971.

YOUR HOLY DNA STIMULUS SUMMARIZED

Every man and woman created by God has a holy DNA that carries spiritual resources and potential to equip them for great service in the world.

Individuals may freely tap into this great potential via prayer, the Scriptures, and the leading of the Holy Spirit of God.

Unlike genetic DNA, one's holy DNA coding can be upgraded when we are made new (surrender to Jesus as Lord) and choose to follow Christ. Old negative things pass away, and new positive character traits emerge. "Yet to all who received him, to those who believed in his name, he gave the right to become children of God" (John 1:12).

SPIRITUAL BLIND DATES

And he sent a man before them—Joseph, sold as a slave.
—Psalm 105:17

I DROVE AN hour to Raleigh one day to conduct some family business. Afterward, I found myself with five hours to kill. I drove by a cinema looking for a popular movie, but it was R-rated, so I substituted a little-heard-of PG film called "Eight Below." It seemed more appropriate for a Christian's viewing. Little did I know God was setting me up for a blind date.

The movie was a mushy story about eight sled dogs stranded in the North Pole in the dead of winter and trying to survive the arctic cold. Although I was never much of an animal lover, the story deepened my appreciation for dogs. I returned home to Fayetteville the next day and urged my wife to see the movie. A few days later, she fell in love with the sled dogs—hook, line, and sinker. Tears streamed down her cheeks as six dogs survived and were rescued from the wild. Two died during the ordeal.

A week later, a stray dog with long brown hair, looking somewhat like one of the dogs in the movie, showed up in our yard one evening. A Shepherd-Chow mix, she darted from the back corner of our driveway, licking and jumping on us.

"Get him off of me!" my wife screamed. "Get down! No! No! Stop! Will you get that dog away from here?" Anne was not fond of dogs. She and her mother's pet dog Puff shared a mutual hatred of each other during Anne's childhood years.

The next day, the large, playful puppy greeted us again, ignoring our previous negative reactions. We refused to feed her for two days, hoping she would disappear, but her affections never abated. By day three, I placed some water in a bowl and left her a few scraps from our table. It seemed to me that she flashed a big smile across her autumn brown face framed by two floppy ears.

By the fourth day, I gave in and opened a can of dog food.

"You've got to call the pound, dad," my son PJ suggested. "You know mother hates dogs. She's afraid of them." So, the next day I called the county dog catcher. When the officer arrived, the husky puppy nervously whined and pulled away from her rope and even urinated in the street. The dog catcher finally lifted her into his truck and fastened the cage. I felt horrible, like Benedict Arnold, as she rode away captive.

Two days later, I still felt like a villain, while my family turned against me.

"You know, I think we ought to get the dog back," my son said one evening.

"Yeah, I bet she was terrified when that truck came. Poor dog," my wife added.

I wanted to strangle them, but they badgered me until I consented to retrieve the dog.

"But you all have to go get her!" I demanded. "I'm not doing your dirty work again." The next day she returned to our driveway. We named her Myra.

Where did she come from? Who dropped her in our neighborhood? Why did she decide to camp by our trash can? Scores of other houses dotted our neighborhood, so why ours?

God set us up! Without a doubt, I was completely convinced of it.

Believe me, I knew all about pet setups. Many years ago, my other son CJ came home grinning after an elementary school carnival. He carefully held two small white containers the size of Chinese takeout cartons. Excitedly, he announced he had won two goldfish.

"Oh, NO!" I protested to no avail. And amazingly, both fish lived more than five years. I became their primary caregiver, feeding them and cleaning the fish bowl day after day; taking the fish with us on trips and vacations and nursing them back to health on many occasions. I have borne the brunt of many pet setups.

Just a few years ago, someone asked us to keep a cat until they could move to another state. But they never returned! We got stuck with her 'till death (hers) did we part. That flimflam became a two-year feline project costing hundreds of dollars of pet food, vet care, and tags. We even endured household discord because the cat loved my wife and hated me.

My mantra became "No more pets! No more pets!" I was immunized against any adopt-a-pet plan. But I never suspected God. The Lord was smooth, and I didn't see it coming. God arranged that dog-gone blind date. It was one of those divine appointments that the Creator concocts every now and then. I believe God gets a big kick out of many of these surprises.

If God used ravens to feed the prophet Elijah (1 Kings 17:4), arranged a donkey for Jesus' entry into Jerusalem on Palm Sunday, used a talking donkey to interrupt Balaam's journey to curse Israel (Num. 22:28), and allowed a crowing rooster to reveal the apostle Peter's denial of Jesus (Mark 14:30,66-72), then surely God could place a dog in my path! Myra needed a home and even looked like a small version of the lead dog actress in the movie. I was ripe for the picking.

More importantly, God knew we needed Myra. Every day my wife and I take her on mile-long walks, a much-needed benefit to our health. Also, our getting an unending supply of face licks and her getting belly rubs provides us with vital anti-stress therapy.

Back to the Word: Spiritual Blind Dates

Does our Lord prep us for new events? Does God arrange divine appointments for us? Of course he does.

Scripture reveals that the Lord "sent a man before them—Joseph, sold as a slave." The king sent for him and released him, and then made Joseph master of his household and ruler over all he possessed (Ps. 105:17, 20-21). Joseph's brothers left him to die in a big pit one day, and slave traders passed by finding him still alive. Joseph became a slave in Egypt, was imprisoned, and finally was set free. He then became a prince under the Pharaoh of Egypt, with authority over the food stores of the nation. Then famine struck Canaan and the people of Israel fled to Egypt, where Joseph fed his brothers and the whole nation from the Pharaoh's storehouses. What a blind date! Joseph and his brothers never imagined they would set eyes upon one another again.

The psalmist lets us know that the brothers meant their deed for evil, but God turned it to good. God is constantly preparing us for blind dates (divine appointments) that profoundly change our lives and grow our faith.

God can intervene in our lives without our knowledge and destine us to encounter special people or situations that can alter our lives. I call these spiritual blind dates. They are arranged meetings with something or someone we were not expecting

A Marriage Made in Heaven

In the Old Testament book of Ruth, when Ruth left the land of Moab with her mother-in-law Naomi, they both had lost husbands and fallen into poverty. They traveled by foot to live in Naomi's hometown, Bethlehem of Judea, where Ruth gleaned leftover grain in the fields. God was only prepping Ruth to meet Boaz, her family redeemer. Boaz owned the field and heard of Ruth's faithfulness to his relative Naomi. Upon seeing her working so hard, he showed her great favor and married her.

God prepared their hearts for each other. It was a marriage made in heaven. Ruth and Boaz gave birth to Obed, the father of Jesse, who became the father of Israel's King David. More astounding, this family line led to the birth of Jesus Christ in Bethlehem many years later. The point is that sometimes the Lord prepares us for unexpected events, people, and life changes that will benefit us.

A Blind Roadside Date

Remember blind Bartimaeus in the gospel of Mark? As Jesus left the town of Jericho with his disciples, a large crowd followed. Bartimaeus sat beside a road begging. Someone in the crowd told him that Jesus was passing by, so he began shouting, "Jesus, Son of David, have mercy on me!" (10:47). Others tried to hush him, but he kept crying out loudly until he received the Master's close attention. Then Bartimaeus asked Jesus to restore his sight.

Jesus said "Go, your faith has healed you." And "immediately he received his sight and followed Jesus along the road" (10:52). We never know when God will put us in a particular place, at a particular time, with a particular person, and in a particular situation for our benefit. But when the opportunity knocks, we can cry out and ask God to help us receive the blessing. Don't be shy. Jesus can open doors nobody can shut, but we must be willing and ready to walk into his favor.

A Botched Blind Date

Such was not the case with the rich young ruler who met Jesus one day. The story is recorded in the tenth chapter of Mark. The Savior invited the young man to follow him, but he refused. The young man had great wealth, which kept him from immediate discipleship. His blind date with Jesus was botched. Soon afterward, Jesus told his disciples, "It is easier for a camel to go through the eye of a needle than for a rich man to enter the kingdom of God" (10:25). How often do poor and marginalized people in society respond to Jesus sooner than the rich and powerful? Could that be why Jesus' twelve disciples were plain, ordinary men?

Could it be that America's recent economic mess occurred because we were too rich for too long? Were we in love with money so much we failed to see God? Did we miss divine appointments because we chased silver and gold? By the world's standards, the vast majority of our nation's citizens are rich. But such abundance may blind us from following Jesus. Do we put comfort and ease before serving the Lord? Have we put our money to good use for

God's kingdom, or only for our personal fiefdoms? Have we botched any of our divine appointments?

What keeps us from really following Jesus today? Could it be friends, fun, career, procrastination, ambition, intellect, social status, busyness, sex, money, or some other distraction? The disciples witnessed many divine appointments and awesome miracles with Jesus. After the encounter with the young ruler they asked Jesus, "Then who can be saved?" Jesus said, "With man this is impossible, but not with God; all things are possible with God" (Mark 10:27).

The A-Team Example

Do you remember the A-Team on TV? The main character would always say, "I love it when a plan comes together." God's plans surely come together in God's time for God's people. So keep your spirit connected to the Holy Spirit. God's blind dates are meant for your good.

Be serious about following Jesus just like Bartimaeus. He wanted more than a handout. What about us? What do we want from Jesus? Is it merely a handout, or just some material desire, or do we want to be Christ's disciple?

Bartimaeus' faith made him well. His faith was that things would get better when he came to Jesus. Grab hold of some Bartimaeus faith! Leap up from your needy beggar position and run to Jesus. Believe things will get better.

How many times have we felt crucified, abandoned, and nailed down by an inescapable worldly crisis? Maybe God was prepping us for something big, perhaps some better days to come. When Jesus went into the wilderness at about thirty years of age, he faced three temptations from the Devil (Matt. 4:1-11). God was prepping his Son for the great ministry of salvation.

Other Biblical Blind Dates

When God called Abraham from his homeland and told him to offer a sacrifice when no animal was in sight (only his son Isaac stood nearby), God was prepping Abraham to lead a nation that would rival the stars in the sky. Abraham had faith that better days would come.

When the king of Persia snatched Esther from her Jewish family and forced her to become the state's queen, God was prepping her to save the Jews from Haman's genocidal plot. Her cousin, Mordecai, challenged her to intervene. She risked her life to save her people, hoping better days would come. The antagonist, Haman, had a divine blind date with the gallows.

When Hosea was told by God to marry a prostitute, the prophet sorrowed, but God prepped Hosea to preach to Israel about their unfaithfulness to the Lord. The prophet clung to hope that better days were coming.

The years young David spent in the back-breaking labor of tending his father's sheep forced the lad to kill lions and bears to protect the flock. God prepared the future king to one day meet Goliath and defend the honor of Israel.

And when Jesus knew that he faced death on a cruel Roman cross, he said, "I tell you the truth: It is for your good that I am going away. Unless I go away, the Counselor will not come to you; but if I go, I will send him to you" (John 16:7). Then he said, "But when he, the Spirit of truth, comes, he will guide you into all truth. He will not speak on his own; he will speak only what he hears, and he will tell you what is yet to come" (16:13). Jesus prepared his disciples for the Holy Spirit's coming. The Spirit was to be their helper, and Jesus knew that better days were coming when God's Spirit would be poured out on all flesh willing to believe and receive him, and that everyone who calls on the name of the Lord will be saved (Acts 2:17-21).

Two of the greatest blind dates in all of history appeared at the cross of Christ. Two thieves, nailed to crosses on each side of Jesus, never suspected an encounter with the Son of God. One rejected God's son and perished. The other accepted Jesus and asked to be remembered when Jesus entered his kingdom. Jesus replied, "I tell you the truth, today you will be with me in paradise" (Luke 23:43). Have you accepted or rejected your divine encounters? We all need to take advantage of our spiritual blind dates.

Go and Do Likewise

In 1980, my father retired from a thirty-nine-year pastorate. Some people looked to me for the church's future. Others looked elsewhere. For weeks I did not apply for the position, hoping to avoid the evolving schism. I prayed that God would allow that cup to pass, but the Master said no. Obediently, I placed my name into consideration for the office of pastor.

Three names were presented to fill the pastorate, and hundreds showed up on election night to choose a pastor. A vote ensued and I finished a close second. Relieved that the church struggle ended, I nevertheless felt the pain of rejection. I recalled Jesus saying, "A prophet is honored everywhere except his own country" (John 4:44, NLT), so I tried taking consolation in those words but to no avail.

"Lord," I shouted within, "I wanted no part of this!" The next few days grew testier as anger and grief ravaged my family. I publicly greeted one "I'm sorry" after another with humility, but I had endured just about enough of humility. Some folks expressed real concern while others gloated. Much like Job, I grew sick of everyone's advice.

Little did I know that God was preparing me and that better days were coming. A wonderful blind date waited if I was willing to walk into my destined favor by faith.

The week after the vote, my wife saw a notice in the state's Baptist paper advertising a media position for a Christian citizens' anti-hunger advocacy group in Washington, D.C., called Bread for the World. She urged me to apply. Plenty of tough competition arose for that job, but one of my references—an exemplary educator and pastor named Dr. Frank B. Weaver—painted such a glowing picture of me that I was hired.

I did not possess the administrative skills needed to pastor a large church when my dad retired. The Lord shielded me from that kind of failure. But God wanted me to bear my cross during the pastor selection process. It strengthened me for better days ahead. The job at Bread for the World taught me many supervisory skills that I now use to lead a twelve hundred-member church about a sixty-minute drive south of my dad's old congregation.

The Bible says, "And we know that in all things God works for the good of those who love him, who have been called according to his purpose....And those he predestined, he also called; those he called, he also justified; those he justified, he also glorified" (Rom. 8:28-30).

Indeed, God had First Baptist Church in Fayetteville (NC) in mind for me all along, even when I got shipped off to Washington. A blind date awaited me down the road. God knew better days were coming. Bread for the World gave me an opportunity to travel overseas, and since then I have learned to embrace those spiritual blind dates more eagerly.

When God opens a door of opportunity for you, be prepared and eager to go through!

REFLECTION/DISCUSSION

1. Do you feel the story about the dog was a divine setup? Why or why not?
2. Has God ever set you up, ever arranged a blind date for your life, by placing people or circumstances in your path unexpectedly that were for your benefit? What happened?
3. Blind Bartimaeus called out to Jesus for mercy and help. What did he want? Did he get it? What have you wanted from Jesus? Have you gotten it? Why or why not?
4. Sometimes people cry out for Jesus' help but want it on their own terms. Bartimaeus could have only wanted a handout of food or money instead of his sight. When you cry out to God, are you looking for a handout or for a closer walk with the Lord? Do you underestimate what God can do? Why are we sometimes afraid of what Jesus offers us?
5. The Rich Young Ruler's blind date with Jesus went bad. Have you ever walked away from the Lord's offer to you? Did you later regret it?
6. The story of Bartimeaus shows us that Jesus' own disciples were blind. In the tenth chapter of Mark, Jesus told them that he would suffer and die in Jerusalem, but they could

not see this divine appointment with death. Do you see the full scope of Jesus or do you see the parts you like most? What parts of Jesus' life and character disturb you?

7. If the rich young man had seen who Jesus really was, would he have made a different decision? Are there things you would have done differently in life years ago if you had known Jesus as you do today?

8. The young ruler and Bartimaeus responded to their blind dates with Jesus very differently. So did the two thieves who hung on crosses next to Jesus. Who are you most like, Bartimaeus, the young ruler, or one of the thieves? Maybe there's another biblical character that depicts your relationship with God. Who is it and what makes him or her like you?

9. Jesus told the blind man that his faith had made him well. How strong is your faith in Jesus Christ? What will you do to increase your faith?

OUTREACH MINISTRY ACTIVITY

What has God called you to do that takes you out of your comfort zone and requires great faith? Is it to help someone you really do not like very much? Is it to go the second and third miles with people who bring you grief? Is it to be kind to a great sinner? Has God asked you to serve in a ministry that you have avoided? Do you witness to others about Jesus and share your faith? Move outside your box and do the will of the Lord. There are several evangelism programs that teach Christians to share their faith in a toxic world. First (Missionary) Baptist Church in Fayetteville uses the FAITH program available from LifeWay Christian Resources. Find a program because God wants you to be a loving witness.

Also, FBC participates in the Interfaith Hospitality Network of churches feeding and sheltering homeless families. We often encounter spiritual blind dates while hosting these families. We take time with them to share our faith and hope in Jesus Christ. There may be a similar ministry in your area that your church can support.

SPIRITUAL BLIND DATES SUMMARIZED

God sets us up with blind dates and divine appointments every now and then. You never know when he will put you in a particular place, at a particular time, with a particular person, or for a particular reason.

God is constantly preparing us for great opportunities in life. Sometimes our preparation is painful but necessary. He knows that better days are coming for us even when we can't see them.

The light of God's divine love will help us discern divine opportunities. We must allow our minds and spirits to be vigilant and to walk through these doors.

When asking God for help, ask for more than a handout. Seek a new life and greater discipleship that bring you victory in a toxic world.

HOT TIPS FROM THE BIG BAILOUT!

It is finished!
—John 19:30

JUST A COUPLE of years out of college I landed a pretty good job as the sports information director at N.C. A&T State University in Greensboro. During my first season, I published the top college football magazine in America (Division II schools). The university rewarded me with a trip to the College Sports Information Directors national convention in New Orleans.

I flew down to the Big Easy for the first time and checked into a very nice hotel on Bourbon Street. Looking out over the French Quarter from my hotel room balcony that first evening, I was amazed as large crowds gathered. I heard tantalizing and alluring sounds that I had never heard before in my life. Surely, I concluded, Christians can have a little fun.

A curious twenty-two-year old single man with time to kill, I joined the masses on the street below to get an up-close feel for the ever-increasing merriment. Jazz music blared from night clubs' open doors as people laughed and drank plenteously. Alcohol seemed to be a prerequisite for a good time. Overhead, a nude manikin darted in and out from the second floor window of a corner bar. Skimpily dressed revelers wearing colorful outfits whizzed by me with each step. I told myself that Christians, too, must sometimes experience new things and places in order to help fallen humanity. But admittedly, my mind was far from ministry or serving God. The glitz of Bourbon Street pulled me into some lewd underworld territory of the Devil. The frivolity only masked Satan's cunning purpose.

The revelry reached a fever pitch around midnight as I walked block after block into unexplored territory. Then I looked up and noticed a big wooden cross in the middle of the street. A few folks held it up and passed out literature. What a sight. In the middle of a mess, at the center of mayhem, lust, porn, and depraved partying, there was a cross. A cross stood boldly for the Savior of the world. I walked reverently around it and headed back toward my hotel room. It sent a most timely reminder to my soul: "Where can I go from your Spirit? Where can I flee from your presence? If I go up to the heavens, you are there; if I make my bed in the depths, you are there" (Ps. 139:7-8). No one can hide from God.

Here a large replica of the cross of Christ stood amidst thousands traveling in the wrong direction. Some people that night never knew Jesus Christ. Some heard a little about him, but had no close relationship with the Lord. Others, maybe like me, after momentarily losing their way, needed redirection, repentance, or turning. I thank the Lord for that cross and the Christians in the middle of Bourbon Street at midnight.

BACK TO THE WORD: HOT TIPS FROM THE BIG BAILOUT!

Much like I walked around that cross in New Orleans, let us walk around Calvary today in our hearts, minds, and spirits, allowing the crucifixion of Jesus Christ to redirect us toward victorious living in a new decade. Here are some valuable tips from my making such a journey.

Hot Tip #1—The Word of Despair

"And at the ninth hour Jesus cried out with a loud voice, 'Eloi, Eloi, lama sabachthani?'—which means, 'My God, my God, why have you forsaken me?'" (Mark 15:34)? This statement conveys the deep, deep despair of Jesus hanging on the cross just outside Jerusalem. Darkness overshadowed the crucifixion scene. Nailed to a wooden cross between two common criminals, Jesus felt physical and spiritual despair. Much of his pain came from his feelings of abandonment and forsakeness. Soldiers gambled for his clothes and various enemies in the crowd tormented him. Friends deserted him and his Father in heaven allowed him to suffer. But remember, when we feel forsaken and abandoned, our greatest victory may be just a breath away.

The words Jesus spoke from the cross that day give us some crucial guidance in a dangerous and uncertain world. Many have felt tormented by national events in the past decade since 9/11. But nothing compares to Jesus, who felt enormous agony while bearing our sins at Calvary. So let us hear more of his dying words. They comprise his last will and testament, and as those words led him to overcome death, they will do the same for us.

Hot Tip #2—The Word of Forgiveness

"Father, forgive them, for they do not know what they are doing" (Luke 23:34). The Octomom: Father forgive her for foolishly miscalculating the cost of motherhood. Bernie Madoff: Father, give him a contrite heart and forgive him for his greed and reckless destruction of so many people's lives. Those bank executives and corporate CEOs who have used wicked schemes to steal billions of dollars: Father, please convict their hearts and forgive them for their sins. Let them no longer pocket multi-million dollar bonuses while average citizens struggle to live.

This statement of Christ from the cross asking his Father in heaven to forgive us is a magnanimous prayer of intercession. Jesus prayed for his tormentors and adversaries, both Jew and Gentile. *Americans desperately need to hear this Word*, for we must pray for our adversaries, both foreign and domestic. We cannot rush to war after every affront, after every shoe bomb and underwear bomb attempt on our airlines.

Forgive the Christian pastor who prayed for President Obama's death and for his consignment to hell. Forgive Christians for laughing with late night TV talk show host David Letterman when he joked about Sarah Palin's pregnant daughter (later admitting that he had sex with women employees of his show). Forgive John Edwards for his infidelity to his sick wife. Forgive Tiger Woods and hope that he finds a moral and spiritual compass in Jesus Christ, who can lead him to greatness again. Indeed, too much hatred, condemnation, and injustice surfaced in America in recent years, undermining our nation. We poisoned ourselves as surely as Jim Jones' venomous Kool Aide killed hundreds of U.S. citizens in Guyana in 1978.

Jesus warned us, "Stop judging others, and you will not be judged." He said, "Whatever measure you use in judging others, it will be used to measure how you are judged" (Matt. 7:1-2, NLT). Remember, when your index finger points at someone else, three other fingers point back at you. Harsh and unforgiving attitudes cripple our society, and forgiveness does not come easily.

An elderly African wise man was asked one day to visit another village and judge someone's wrongs. He hesitated, but after great urging, he took the trip. Upon entering the village, people noticed he was lugging a leaking bucket of water tied to a rope on the ground behind him.

"Why are you dragging that water bucket full of holes?" a villager inquired.

"You have asked me to judge someone else today," he said, "but my sins leak out behind me."

How have we disobeyed and dishonored Jesus? How have we crucified our Lord by our foolish ways? How have we hurt the cause of Jesus Christ and driven nails into his hands and feet? Before we condemn others so vehemently, we need to take a look at ourselves. We need to find room in our hearts to forgive. No truer words than these have been written: "Therefore, there is now no condemnation for those who are in Christ Jesus" (Rom. 8:1). We are forgiven and given eternal life. We need to hear this message from the cross today.

Hot Tip #3—The Word of Salvation

"I tell you the truth, today you will be with me in paradise" (Luke 23:43). Hallelujah! God's forgiveness is for all people, and it is instantaneous. Salvation is for all people. In the previous statement from the cross, Jesus prayed for the forgiveness of all humanity. With this utterance the Lord demonstrated forgiveness. He offered salvation to a thief on a cross beside him that very same day!

This thief was obviously a scourge to society and a malefactor. Yet he represented all of us, "for all have sinned and fall short of the glory of God" (Rom. 3:23).

As followers of Jesus Christ, we must not simply be hearers of the words found in the Bible, but also be doers of the Word. Jesus did something. In this case he forgave a repentant thief and saved a dying sinner.

We are all thieves. When we sin, we rob from God. We steal from the very character of Christ's church and our sins do great harm to ourselves and others. In which ways have we been thieves?

When we lie, we have stolen from truth.
When we cheat, we have stolen from honesty.
When we lust, we have stolen from purity.
When we gossip, we have stolen from someone's reputation.
When we get jealous, we have damaged true love.
When we are judgmental, we steal from mercy.
When we commit adultery, we steal someone's husband or wife.
When we are gluttons, we steal from our health and disrespect
    our bodies (the temples of God).
When we are selfish, we steal from generosity.
When we are hateful, we disturb the peace.
When we curse, we rob from decency.
When we are lazy, we rob productivity.
When we are prejudiced, we diminish humanity.
When we are unfair, we disrupt justice.
When we are angry, we steal from joy.
When we are negative, we rob faith.
When we are stubborn, we block forgiveness.

We are all robbers and thieves, but thank God we are forgiven. When we are unforgiving, we wrestle against the kingdom of God. There are too many robbers in America picking people's pockets. We should all be under spiritual arrest. We are all thieves, and we are all guilty. Hands up!

Thank God, Jesus Christ forgives us and promises us eternal life (heaven) if we trust and follow him. This is the gracious Word of Salvation. Receive it joyfully. The Gospel of John reminds us, "To all who received him, to those who believed in his name, he gave the right to become children of God" (1:12). We can all be in paradise with Christ Jesus our Lord. We must not stop at simply believing in Christ, for even the demons do that. Rather, we must receive Jesus into our hearts and allow him to abide with us.

Hot Tip #4—The Word of Affection

"When Jesus saw his mother there, and the disciple whom he loved standing nearby, he said to his mother, 'Dear woman, here is your son,' and to the disciple, 'Here is your mother.' From that time on, this disciple took her into his home" (John 19:26-27). In the midst of the biggest crime in world history, while being crucified for the sins of the world and with extreme pain racking his body and spirit, Jesus took time to care for his mother and show her genuine affection.

While we suffer, let us care for others. While we recover from economic recession and gloom, let us not turn *on* each other but turn *to* each other. Never be too busy for a gesture of compassion. As Christians our purpose is to serve. Servants sacrifice themselves for the good of others.

What love Jesus demonstrated. In his time of greatest need, the Son of Man cared for his mother. We can do nothing as important as trying to emulate our Savior. Notice jobless people, struggling senior citizens, youth needing mentors, and homeless people needing shelter. When we see hungry people, or mothers and fathers hurting, or husbands and wives in trouble, we need to lend a helping hand. Notice lonely people and the disrespected man or woman and go to them. Focus on the lost and the unsaved—focus on somebody other than yourself. Be a cross bearer in the middle of your own Bourbon street.

There was a little girl, about six years old, who once carried a toddler around a church picnic area for more than an hour one hot summer day. The little boy kept sliding down her hip and she kept pulling him back up as she walked. A deacon asked, "Can I help you hold the boy for a while? He must be heavy."

She replied, "He ain't heavy, he's my brother."

Americans urgently need to heed Jesus' word of affection. We are our brothers' and sisters' keepers. How can we stand idly by while millions are without food and shelter, health care and jobs, or without decent education and clothes? Jesus commended his obedient followers saying, "for I was hungry and you gave me something to eat, I was thirsty and you gave me something to drink, I was a stranger and you invited me in, I needed new clothes and you clothed me, I was sick and you looked after me, I was in prison and you came to visit me" (Matt. 25:35-36). Can we say we have faith in God without proving it by our actions and affections for one another? We must forever seek to comfort and aid those in need, and to always leave room for Christ's compassion in our hearts.

Hot Tip #5—The Word of Triumph

"It is finished." (John 19:30). This is Jesus' word of victory from the cross, where he proclaimed the completion of the *biggest bailout* in world history. When we are down and out, do we trust the plan of God to give us victory? Redemption means that a debt has been paid off. If you take your watch to a pawnbroker, you can redeem it by paying off the debt. In a manner similar to the way Wall Street was bailed out for bad financial practices in 2008 and 2009, Jesus rescued us from our bad spiritual practices. "For God so loved the world that he gave his one and only Son, that whoever believes in him shall not perish but have eternal life. For God did not send his Son into the world to condemn the world, but to save the world through him (John 3:16-17).

The greatest bailout was not to AIG, Citicorp, Goldman Sachs, Bank of America, or any other large banks on Wall Street. That bailout was in the billions of dollars, but God's bailout rescued billions of people of every nation and tribe down through the ages. Christ's bailout for us at the cross was priceless. Money could not buy our salvation. "Though he was God, he did not demand and cling to his rights as God. He made himself nothing; he took the humble position of a slave and appeared in human form. And in human form he obediently humbled himself even further by dying a criminal's death on a cross" (Phil. 2:6-8, NLT).

Jesus put one hundred percent of his skin into God's salvation plan. He did not come down from that cross until God's plan was finished. It was a one hundred percent bailout for all humanity and for all time if only we come to God by faith in his Son Jesus Christ. This bailout should go into the Guinness book of records because it will never be surpassed in size or quality. Furthermore, it perpetually benefits the masses of the world day after day.

This bailout was a gift from God. "For it is by grace you have been saved, through faith—and this not from yourselves, it is the gift of God" (Eph. 2:8). We could not save ourselves, so Jesus sacrificed his life one hundred percent for our souls to be with him in paradise. "The Word became flesh and made his dwelling place among us...full of grace and truth" (John 1:14). Let me ask my readers a question: Have you made a sincere faith commitment to the Lord yet?

Jesus died to save our toxic assets! He paid the price at Calvary for our spiritual bailout with his own life, and his life is the only sacrifice for our sins. Never before and never again, once and for all time, Jesus was God's free gift of eternal life to all humanity.

Hot Tip #6—The Word of Committal

Then Jesus cried out his final Word from the cross, "Father, into your hands I commit my spirit" (Luke 23:46). We must commit our ways to the Lord Jesus Christ and we must dedicate (or re-dedicate) our lives to him. God awaits our genuine commitment to follow Jesus and to live as devoted disciples of the Lord.

Go and Do Likewise

Jesus did not die just for his mother or for the twelve disciples he loved so much. He died for all lost people, including the ones who hated him most and despised his teachings—then and now. The challenge of the church today is to be compassionate toward ungodly people. In the midst of the evils of this present age and the hostilities in a world seemingly gone crazy, the cross of Christ stands in our midst like it did on that New Orleans street. The message of the cross must not be diluted by politics, nationalism, patriotism, capitalism, sexism, militarism, homophobia, racism, materialism, socialism, or religious self-righteousness. God is neither a Republican nor a Democrat. God is totally sovereign!

The church must love and reach out to all people in a broken and hurting world, including the rich and poor, educated and street smart, young and old, and the famous and outcast. We must love and extend God's grace to all races, all classes, and people from all walks of life. The entire human race is invited to shelter under God's big tent.

"Enlarge the place of your tent, stretch your tent curtains wide, do not hold back; lengthen your cords, strengthen your stakes. For you will spread out to the right and to the left ..." (Isa. 54:2-3). It was at the cross that God widened the tent of salvation to all humanity who are willing to come out of darkness and dwell in his marvelous light.

Hot Tip #7—The Word of Fellowship

Christians, love your fellowship with Christ and with your brothers and sisters in the church. While this command to love one another is challenging, it is the demand of discipleship. "Therefore, as we have opportunity, let us do good to all people, especially to those who belong to the family of believers" (Gal. 6:10). We must not take lightly our church or faith community's fellowship. Jesus' agonizing cry from the cross demonstrated God's awesome love. The Son greatly valued fellowship with the Father and with us, and when it was taken away, he felt forsaken and abandoned. He was wounded for our transgressions, bruised for our iniquities, and by his stripes we are healed (Isa. 53).

We must cherish the old rugged cross and highly esteem our co-laborers with Christ. We must nurture our church fellowship, guard and support it, and be partners with others in God's great earthly enterprise. The self-denial Jesus displayed on the cross should be our attitude today (Phil. 2:6). We should all sacrificially value our Christian fellowship, because Christ gave his very life for it.

The love of Christ overcame cliques and rivalries, hatred and malice, divisions and hostilities. This is the challenge of the church in this new decade, to convince the unconvinced of every background that Jesus Christ is Lord! This can be achieved if we greatly value our oneness with God and each other. The church can have great impact in the world only through a deep and abiding desire to sustain its unique fellowship with Almighty God.

Keep these seven hot tips in your hearts and minds as you press on toward the high calling of Christ Jesus. I returned to New Orleans more than two decades later for the Lott Carey Foreign Mission Convention, and I returned to Bourbon Street. This time I was not dazzled by the frivolity and I was not tempted by the debauchery. I wanted to see if that cross was still borne by some determined Christians in the middle of Bourbon Street. It was.

Go and do likewise.

REFLECTION/DISCUSSION

1. When have you cried out in despair? Did you feel that anyone heard you? How do you think Jesus felt on the cross?
2. Can you forgive people who do terrible things? Are there examples of people you would never forgive? Is forgiveness difficult for you? Why? Would God forgive the people you named?
3. If all people have robbed God in some way, that includes you. How are you guilty? Review the list of stolen items in this stimulus chapter and see which ones match you.

4. Despite our ungodly transgressions, Jesus purchased our place in heaven. What do you think about this big bailout for our sins?

5. Who do you need to show more loving affection for among your associates? Will you do it?

6. Have you truly committed your ways to Christ as he committed himself to us? Have you surrendered your life to him? Why or why not?

7. How can you and your group foster greater fellowship in your church? If you don't have a church or faith community, pray for one and let Christ help you find it.

8. Find a large cross on a lawn somewhere in a town, city, or rural area. It may be at a church or cemetery. During a quiet and peaceful time, walk around it several times while meditating on the last words of Jesus Christ. Pause in silence for a minute after meditating on each phrase. What does the Holy Spirit place in your mind and spirit? Close out your study time with prayer. If you are in a study group, come together and share your feelings and insights. How were you inspired by your walk around the cross?

9. Discuss the meaning of Romans 12:1-2. What are good ways to be "living sacrifices" to God in our time?

OUTREACH MINISTRY ACTIVITY

Grief is a very tough time in people's lives. Very often, when people have lost someone very special or something important, tears and emotions overwhelm them. Give aid and comfort to those who are grieving the death of a relative or friend, to someone who has lost a job, or to a person who lost a spouse due to divorce. Aid persons or families who are homeless or who have lost a house to foreclosure. Give comfort to someone who has lost their health or independence. Set up a grief support group in your church or volunteer to help a hospice or meals-on-wheels organization. Follow the pattern of the Savior in giving aid and comfort—not once, but on an ongoing basis. Be an encouraging word from the cross in the middle of Bourbon Street in your community.

HOT TIPS STIMULUS SUMMARIZED

Before vehemently condemning others, let us look at ourselves and find room in our hearts to forgive. Remember, when your index finger points at someone else, three other fingers point back at you.

We're all thieves and there are too many robbers in America picking each other's pockets.

Jesus put one hundred percent of his heart and soul into our spiritual bailout, rescuing us from our toxic assets.

It was the cross of Christ that widened the tent of God's family to all humanity. We must value our Christian fellowship because Christ gave his life for it.

PART THREE

TRY ONE AND FEEL BETTER IN THE MORNING

HARMONY SHOUT-OUT

> How wonderful it is when kindred live
> together in harmony!
> —Psalm 133:1 (NRSV)

*S*OJOURNERS MAGAZINE PUBLISHED a story in 2009 about an American banjo virtuoso named Bela Fleck, who took his instrument back to its roots in Gambia, West Africa. A stringed instrument called the *akonting* probably departed on a slave ship from the Gambian port of Banjul more than a century and a half ago. Fleck "developed the suspicion that some of the greatest acoustic music on earth is hidden in the small villages of Africa."[1]

While in Gambia, Fleck saw a black man split a dried gourd, stretch an animal skin tight across it, construct an akonting before his very eyes, and play it similar to Appalachian old-time banjo musicians back home. Fleck realized that this African instrument became the emblem of the virtually all-white country music culture in America.[2]

The banjo transcended race, continent, color, culture, and nationality. Just as Fleck celebrated the transcontinental connections of the banjo, Americans need to celebrate the universal roots of harmony in all of humanity. Physically, people from all nations and tribes are ninety-nine percent the same material stuff: oxygen, carbon, hydrogen, nitrogen, calcium, and phosphorus. The Bible says God "made every nation of men, that they should inhabit the whole earth; and he determined the times set for them and the exact places where they should live" (Acts 17:26).

The biblical heritage of all people can be traced to a single couple—Adam and Eve. The heritage of Jews, Christians, and Muslims goes back to father Abraham. We are one human family. Praise God for this harmony within humanity. "God created man in his own image, in the image of God he created him; male and female he created them" (Gen. 1:27). This common heritage goes back to our creation and we all carry the image of God, though imperfectly, within us: spirituality, personality, holiness, intelligence, freedom, and love.

Our human origins underscore the importance of celebrating harmony. Harmony is a pleasing integration of components and most people share more values in common than we often recognize. These common components can help unify us today.

Harmony elevates humanity just as harmony enhances music. Play the melody of a song and it may sound ordinary, but play the same song with harmony and it often becomes extraordinary. The tune becomes a pleasing integration of sounds. As a nation, let us orchestrate more harmony in our daily lives instead of more destructive discord. Let us produce a more pleasing integration of our people's gifts and talents.

The civil rights movement of the 1960s succeeded because a variety of people came together and participated. The movement attracted clergy and laity, blacks, whites and Jews, men, women and children, Republicans and Democrats, young and old, rich, middle class and poor. Heated differences sometimes arose, but enough people shared a similar focus—freedom for all people from segregation and racial oppression. This common focus undergirded the coalitions that changed America forever.

No Room for a Vandal Mentality

Undoubtedly, candid public debate is healthy in our democracy. We must critically explore all sides of public policies and draw clear distinctions between our opinions. Much vigorous debate surrounded the health care proposals in Congress in 2009 and 2010. While debating, however, we must avoid verbally slashing one another like a vandal knifing a new set of radial automobile tires. If our rhetoric is too shrill, and if it is laced with deep-seated hatreds, the ensuing verbal tug-of-war may shred our democracy. Insults and ugly name-calling can rip us apart like hurricane Katrina ripped apart New Orleans and the Gulf Coast.

Discord levels in our country have risen dramatically after more than two years of nasty national presidential electioneering and the 2008-2009 U.S. economic decline. TV news personalities shouted at each other out of fear and frustration. Our political leaders sailed into deep, uncharted recessionary waters while everyday citizens' tempers rose to code red. Warnings should have been issued by Homeland Security that our heated rhetoric threatened a national implosion. Domestic terrorists like Joseph Stack, who flew his plane into an IRS office in Austin, Texas because he was upset with the U.S. government, may be spurred on by the reckless words from politicians, cable TV and radio talk show hosts, nasty web bloggers, and other angry social networking types.

We watched the "Birthers," the "Deathers," the "Truthers," and the "Shouters" turn up the heat even higher in America. Debate turned to hate, and hate turned into threats of violent insurrection. One protestor came to a picket line in New Hampshire with a gun strapped to his hip. Americans called their adversaries names, anything from Hitler to socialists to Nazis. Dangerous anti-government militia groups arose, one allegedly plotting to gun down city police officers. The American melting pot boiled into threats of violence.

Despite so many Hatfields and McCoys among us, level heads must prevail. Let us all search for common ground despite our differences. "Be self-controlled and alert. Your enemy the devil prowls around like a roaring lion looking for someone to devour. Resist him ..." (1 Pet. 5:8-9). It is important to tone down the tirades and avoid sparking violence by weaker-minded folks. Instead, give harmony a shout-out!

Hee Haw Harmony

Many years ago (1969-1992), *Hee Haw* was a popular television show broadcast from Nashville, Tennessee. Country music and laughter filled the airwaves for sixty minutes each week as people of all races and backgrounds enjoyed the banjo-picking fun. The show appealed to people in big cities as well as in rural areas. Buck Owens and Roy Clark made people laugh together. We could use more Hee Haw harmony and laughter today. The good things we share far outweigh the bad.

Big City Meets the Backwoods

I used to work as the sports information director for Howard University in Washington, D.C. In the 1970s, I accompanied our All-American mile relay team to the college national track championships in Eugene, Oregon. Uncharacteristically, I waited too long to book a hotel room. In haste, I asked an Oregon motel manager where I could stay. He pointed me to Shiloh House, a home for young Christian men who worked at the local logging camps. I took him up on his idea, and for about a week, a black inner-city professional lived with about a dozen all-white outdoors men. We had a ball. The primary thing was that we all loved the Lord, so culture, color, background, and race became secondary. We learned from our differences and discovered our many similarities. We felt a bond as brothers.

BACK TO THE WORD: A SHOUT-OUT FOR HARMONY

Psalm 133 focuses on harmony among family members, but it also applies harmony to the members of the covenant community in Jerusalem—God's chosen people. The psalmist called harmony within the family one of God's blessings: "How wonderful it is when kindred live together in harmony" (133:1, NRSV).

How can we witness to others about the love of God if we fuss and fight unceasingly? How can we advance God's Kingdom on earth if we constantly store up hatred and pull against each other? Can we effectively share the Good News if we are not one in the Spirit?

How often do we kill one another with our words, attitudes, and actions? We do it at church, at home, at work, and in our schools. Some churches have dance groups that minister by using Christian music during worship services. Their liturgy depends upon harmonious choreography. If one dancer falls while the other jumps, or if one goes left while another mistakenly goes right, harmony is broken. Likewise, the Holy Spirit choreographs harmony among believers. From chaos God's Spirit can create harmony. It happened in the beginning, as recorded in the book of Genesis. The Spirit moves us forward together even though we have differing gifts, talents, and approaches to problems.

Consider this conversation between a man's right hand and his left one:

> A man broke his left hand. One night when he couldn't sleep, he imagined a dialogue between his right and left hands. Right hand said, "Left Hand, you are not missed. Everybody's glad it was you that was broken and not me. You are not very important."
>
> Left Hand asked, "How are you superior?"
>
> Right Hand replied, "Why, my owner cannot write a letter without me."
>
> Left Hand: "But who holds the paper on which he writes?"
>
> Right Hand: "Who swings the hammer?"
>
> Left Hand: "Who holds the nail?"
>
> Right Hand: "Who guides the plane when the carpenter smooths a board?"
>
> Left Hand: "Who steadies the board?"
>
> Right Hand: "When our owner walks down the street and lifts his hat to greet someone, which of us does it?"
>
> Left Hand: "Who holds the briefcase while he does it?"[3]

Each of us is special to the Lord. We are different, that is for sure, but no one is greater than anyone else. Our nation needs individual citizens giving their service for the good of all. We must remember to allow our diversity to contribute to harmony and not detract from it.

Jesus Prayed for Harmony

Jesus told his disciples that thieves and robbers attack the flock of God (John 10:7-11). They come to steal and kill and destroy. Today, more thieves and robbers reside among us than pirates off the coast of Somalia. Doing the work of our enemy the Devil, they attack peace, harmony, joy, and fellowship among groups of people. They seek to destroy the fellowship we enjoy with Jesus Christ and our brothers and sisters in the body of Christ (the church). Yes, the Devil is busy, but we must "Resist him, standing firm in the faith" (1 Pet. 5:9).

We can be thankful that Jesus prayed for his disciples' harmony. And his prayer covers his disciples now as it covered his disciples then. The gospel of John reads, "Holy Father, protect them by the power of your name—the name you gave me—so that they may be one as we are one. While I was with them, I protected them and kept them safe by that name you gave me" (John 17:11-12).

Jesus left us with a heavenly coast guard comprising the Holy Spirit and the Word of God. They protect and guide believers in tough times and lead us through the dangerous waters of life. Jesus came to bring us life more abundantly (John 10:10), and the Spirit promotes peace and harmony among us. "When they arrest you," said Jesus, "do not worry about what to say or how to say it. At that time you will be given what to say, for it will not be you speaking, but the Spirit of your Father speaking through you (Matt. 10:19-20). The Spirit and the Bible give us words to speak and direction for our pathway. Stay closely connected to both.

Madea Goes to Jail

In a movie called "Madea Goes to Jail," actor Tyler Perry portrayed a lighthearted but often out-of-control black woman who constantly created havoc. She constantly failed to seek the Lord *first* in her decision-making and problem-solving processes. In one scene, another woman beat Madea to a parking spot at a shopping center. Madea lost it! She found a fork lift truck, picked up the other woman's red sports car, and dropped it crashing to the ground. Before going to prison, she beat up a police officer. Sadly, Madea mostly used the Bible to support her outrageous behavior.

Like the *Hee Haw* TV show, Madea makes us laugh, and more laughter truly is in order today. There "is a time to weep and a time to laugh" (Eccles. 3:4), the Bible reminds us. There is a time for everything. But we do not need laughter that derisively chuckles at the mistakes of others and gleefully snickers at their downfall. Instead, let us cultivate positive humor that lifts the human spirit. Research reveals that laughter lowers blood pressure, strengthens cardiovascular functions, reduces stress, improves circulation, serves as an antioxidant, boosts the immune system, and produces a sense of well-being.[4] Speakers often begin their talks with ice-breaking humor because it promotes a positive shared experience.

Scrooge and Laughter

Think about the Christmas character Ebeneezer Scrooge and his miserable, stingy, and anti-Christmas livelihood. After three spirits (ghosts) visited him while asleep one Christmas eve night and showed him his dismal life, Scrooge was frightened into seeing the many errors of his ways. When he awakened, Scrooge started laughing and enthusiastically committed himself to a new way of life. On Christmas morning, he brimmed with laughter and celebrated Christmas with family and friends. His joy and laughter were contagious. He contributed his money to charities and promoted harmony wherever he went. In just such a way, our laughter can light up a room and produce harmony, if we are willing to indulge. People of God are called to use music, dance, laughter, and other wholesome qualities as ambassadors for harmony.

Ambassadors for Harmony

An ambassador is a high-ranking diplomat, a representative-in-residence from one government to another. We Christians are ambassadors representing the Kingdom of God to the world. Paul said, "We are therefore Christ's ambassadors, as though God were making his appeal through us" (2 Cor. 5:20). As ambassadors, we need to take time discovering the common chords among people and using them for good. We must learn to create order and harmony out of chaos, as God did in the beginning of the world: "Now the earth was formless and empty, darkness was over the surface of the deep, and the Spirit of God was hovering over the waters" (Gen. 1:2). Also, the Bible tells us to "Live in harmony with each other" (Rom. 12:16, NLT).

GO AND DO LIKEWISE

As ambassadors for harmony, let us serve as positive mini-media outlets to the people in our circles of influence. Here are twelve common-ground ideas on which most people can agree. Let these ideas encourage our strides to victory in this new decade.

- Cheer our nation on! Let's stress the "United" States of America while championing civic participation in our democratic process for all U.S. citizens.
- Serve voluntarily. We possess awesome human resources, yet many of those resources remain untapped. Bring out the best in each other. Let us become one of the thousands of points of light brightening the world like the elder President George H. W. Bush has suggested.
- Demand high-quality education. Make our schools and colleges the best in the world.
- Care for vulnerable people and heal people's wounds and hurts. Aid hungry, homeless, and poor people, especially children and seniors. We are no stronger than our weakest links.
- Preserve religious freedom. Insure freedom to worship (or not worship) for all people.
- Respect freedom of speech. Defend people's rights to be heard. But freedom demands responsibility and liberty does not grant license to falsely holler "fire" in a crowded room.
- Support soldiers and military families. They have made enormous sacrifices for us.

- Practice good stewardship of natural resources. Keep America beautiful—from the mountains to the seas.
- Uphold justice everywhere, and extend mercy anywhere.
- Promote love toward all racial, ethnic, gender, age, religious, class, and orientation groups. Do unto others as you would have others treat you.
- Forgive one another. Nobody is right all the time. Be willing to forgive and to be forgiven.
- Believe our best days are yet to come! Like President Barack Obama, always embody the audacity to hope.

Biblical Harmony and Community

This list of common-ground ideas is not exhaustive, and much could be added to it (or taken away from it) at will. Your list will be different from mine. Just remember to keep the list positive. In Paul's letter to the Romans, the Bible gives us another list to aid us in finding harmony. Be sincere...be devoted to one another... honor one another...be joyful in hope...share with God's people... practice hospitality...bless those who persecute you...rejoice with those who rejoice; mourn with those who mourn...live in harmony with one another...be careful to do what is right...live at peace with everyone...do not take revenge...do not be overcome by evil, but overcome evil with good (Rom. 12:9-21).

There will always be excessive and incendiary voices from the extreme fringes of religious as well as irreligious groups. But we need to give harmony a chance by toning down virulent language. This does not come easily because harmony demands hard work, diligence, and perseverance. It is easier to shout and drown out each other! Surely, there will be times when we all suffer relapses to outright conflict, but we all must beware of drifting off into outrageous behavior.

As community ambassadors for harmony, we should pledge to show diplomacy in representing our opinions to others. In the wisdom literature of the Bible, God promises us a blessing for practicing a common-sense, common-ground approach to life: "How good and pleasant it is when kindred dwell together in harmony. It is where the Lord promised to bless the people with life forevermore" (Ps. 133:1-3, NRSV).

If God can make a blessing out of a banjo, he can use us as instruments of his peace. St. Francis of Assisi reminds us of this:

> Lord, make me an instrument of thy peace,
> Where there is hatred, let me sow love,
> Where there is injury, pardon,
> Where there is doubt, faith,
> Where there is despair, hope,
> Where there is darkness, light,
> Where there is sadness, joy.
> O Divine Master, grant that I may not so much seek to be consoled
>   as to console,
> To be understood, as to understand,
> To be loved, as to love.
> For it is in giving that we receive, it is in pardoning that we are
>   pardoned,
> And it is in dying that we are born to eternal life!

Let God use us as instruments connecting people, bringing harmony among people, and bringing out the best in people. Try harmony and feel better in the morning.

REFLECTION/DISCUSSION

1. If you were a musical instrument, which one would you like to be (tuba, French horn, flute, drum, harp, piano, trombone, drum, etc.)? Why did you select that instrument?
2. What can you do in your areas of influence to create harmony among people?
3. Is discord or harmony most dominant in your family, your workplace, and in your church? How can God use you to improve bad situations?
4. What does Psalm 133:2 compare to harmony?
5. What is the significance of dew in Psalm 133:3?

6. If you were evaluated on your performance as an ambassador for Jesus Christ in your community today (2 Cor. 5:20), would you get a raise, be rated average, or get fired? Why?
7. Of the twelve items listed as areas of harmony for all people, which ones do you like most? Least? Why?
8. List three things that you believe ninety percent of people would agree on.
9. How does the Word of God promote harmony? Is harmony always possible? What about respect?

OUTREACH MINISTRY ACTIVITY

During the heart of the heated debate over health care, a church decided to conduct a service of prayers for the President of the United States. They were true to the apostle Paul's instructions to the church: "I urge, then, first of all, that requests, prayers, intercession and thanksgiving be made for everyone—for kings and all those in authority, that we may live peaceful and quiet lives in all godliness and holiness" (1 Tim. 2:1-2). The people of the church felt that the elected leader of our nation needed prayer, regardless of race, gender, age, or political party. The hopes of the people are linked to sound leadership. Whoever is the U.S. president when you read this book, pray for her or him. Lift up your local, state, and national leaders in prayer—even those with whom you may strongly disagree. Consider holding a Pray for Our Leaders Service and invite the whole community. We may not like the choices of some voters, but we live in a democracy, and we must abide by the decisions of the majority. Even if we see leaders as adversaries, the Bible tells us to pray for our enemies. Prayer can heal and promote harmony in the most difficult times.

HARMONY SHOUT-OUT STIMULUS SUMMARIZED

We are ambassadors of harmony, and we must represent the kingdom of God to the world.

Though there will be times when we relapse, harmony demands work, diligence, and perseverance.

God promises a blessing of life forevermore for practicing harmony.

The Holy Spirit gives us words to speak when we are under stress and facing opposition (Matt. 10:19-20).

KINDNESS/VITAMIN K

> If only my master would see the prophet who is in
> Samaria! He would cure him of his leprosy.
> —2 Kings 5:3

A T HIGH NOON in Hampton, Virginia, an overwhelming
impulse rushed over me that I couldn't keep to myself. On the
first Thursday in June, on the fourth day of the Hampton University
Ministers' Conference, thousands of registered participants
streamed from the campus coliseum and scattered throughout the
Tidewater area searching for food. Many headed to restaurants while
others settled for fried fish dinners from local vendors adjacent to
the arena. My wife and I headed to the student dining hall to use
our pre-purchased discounted meal tickets.

Scores of people beat us to the old brick building, so we patiently
stood outside, sweating in the blistering sunshine. After several
minutes, a receptionist hole-punched our tickets just inside the
doors, admitting us to another officially sanctioned lunch time
melee. If *Survivor* needs a wildly challenging location for its tribes
next season, I strongly recommend Cleveland Dining Hall.

Exhaust fans feverishly sucked the smell of fish and cornbread
from the air while hundreds of famished conferees scurried about

collecting their mid-day meals onto brown, time-worn cafeteria trays. Workers, dressed in food-splattered white uniforms, rushed across the floor shoving carts loaded with salad, beans, peas, cheese, and butter. Pots and pans clanged as women with black hair nets dumped fried fish, pork chops, rice, and gravy into hot aluminum bins.

Lunch at Hampton was the five-star meal of the day. The staff whipped up potatoes and fluffed white rice, and they restocked the drink machines with tea, sodas, and juices. They prepared a sumptuous feast for the masses, busily huffing and puffing to satisfy visitors from the four corners of America. We loaded our trays, grabbed our drinks, and tossed our salads, all while scanning the landscape for a spot to sit. Crammed with too many tables and chairs, outdated Cleveland Hall forced Anne and me to squeeze through narrow rows to claim two empty chairs. We carefully avoided dropping our vittles on top of the patrons already eating below.

After twisting into our seats, we declared "mission accomplished." We landed at a table jammed with smiling people who quickly asked our names and, "Where are you all from?" Each day we chatted with strangers until we knew somebody in their town that they knew. [There are only six degrees of separation (or fewer), you know. For example: My (1) wife (2) has a close friend (3) who's mother (4) is a friend to the mother (5) of Denzel Washington (6).]

Cleveland Hall was no place for the quiet and cowardly. Somehow, on the next-to-last day of the conference, we all ate our fill without serious skirmishes, remaining within the borders of chaotic civility. My wife wouldn't pass up this ritual for a million dollars. A social animal, she loves rubbing shoulders and engaging in close-up table talk. It serves her needs more than the meat and potatoes on her plate. Like a goldfish rising to the water's surface for flakes of food dropped into a fishbowl, Anne feasted upon this gregarious super bowl of camaraderie.

The cafeteria workers fearlessly performed their duties as I marveled at the human capacity to eek out a living in such a harsh working environment. They deserved combat pay for heroism.

Now, back to that overwhelming impulse that rushed over me. Suddenly I felt a spontaneous calling to venture into a zone high above the feathery cirrus clouds of summer. The crowd noise and clatter failed to dampen my out-of-the-body rush. I did not blame the Holy Spirit for what was about to go down, nor did I assume that Jesus sanctioned it. Compelled like a child on Christmas morning who is anxious to rip open a big box wrapped in shiny paper with a colorful bow on top, I couldn't resist the urge to unfurl my impulse before the entire cafeteria audience. It was like a burning fire shut up in my bones.

So, I did it! I broke through my thin bubble of sanity. With my peers packed in around me like sardines, and after gulping down a glass of southern brewed sweet tea, I stood on my chair and hopped up onto our table, startling my wife and our newly found dining partners.

"Listen up everybody," I hollered. (I know how to holler 'cause my home, North Carolina, hosts the annual Spivey's Corner national hollering contest. So I shouted louder.) "Listen up! Listen up! These cafeteria workers have served us all week. They've prepared three meals a day, put up with our attitudes, impatience, tempers, whims, and wants. They've been hospitable even when we haven't deserved it."

By now everybody froze in their tracks, like somebody pushed the pause button on a DVD remote control. Eyes focused on me like bank tellers watching a robber. *Has this guy gone postal? Will he pull a gun? Maybe somebody should jump him and call security.* But it happened so fast and they weren't sure how to react. The noisy hall calmed to a whisper.

"We have jumped in front of people rushing to the salad bar," I continued in my booming voice, "left the ice cream maker a mess, dueled for butter and pastries, left mashed potatoes smeared on the floor and crumbs on the tables. Yet, they have served us superbly.

"So at this time, I want everybody to give a big cheer to the cafeteria workers: Hip, hip, hooray!" I chanted. "Hip, hip, hooray! Hip, hip, hooray!" they joined in the chorus with me. "Hip, hip, hooray!" Those eating and being served in line, the ones still at the salad and dessert bars, those at the beverage section, and others dropping off their dirty plates, trays, and silverware, all broke out in a cheer—clapping and hollering in appreciation.

My impulse paid off! So I climbed down from my perch and saw my wife's flushed face as the crowd returned to normal. The noise resumed and laughter filled the place. But if you could have seen the expressions on the workers' faces. Oh, those looks were worth my temporary insanity. Their eyes beamed with delight. Smiles burst across their faces. Their burdens seemed a bit lighter or maybe simply easier to bear. They were more than servants now; they were VIPs.

What if Americans would boldly offer the gift of what I call vitamin K—kindness—to other people more often in our toxic world? How about carrying a vitamin bottle full of kindness each day instead of marching out armed with pills of brutal criticism and scorn?

Random Acts of Kindness

What drove me to such a zany display of public emotion? What energized my hopping up on a table and shouting out to total strangers? Where did that impulse come from? The previous day my wife and I bought a nice thank-you card and sealed it in an envelope with a twenty dollar bill for a cafeteria worker. We did this because we had noticed her upbeat demeanor year after year. She stood out!

At Wednesday evening's meal, we pulled out the card and simply said thanks for making our visits so enjoyable. She paused behind the glass serving table as steam rose from the hot meat loaf and broccoli below. I had never seen her stop working. She labored perpetually with what must have been a supernatural gift for serving food. But for a few seconds, she paused, gripped the card with a big smile, and held up her hands and arms to God. Thanksgiving was painted all over her face as she whispered, "God bless you all. I'll never forget this." Then she shoved the card down in her apron pocket and resumed scooping up food for others behind us.

That look of gratitude made me feel better than all the conference lectures and presentations. Our small gift was a random act of kindness that energized my tabletop performance the next day. I hope it inspired others to make tangible gifts of appreciation to the workers, or at least to act more courteously.

I discovered a new vitamin during that impulse. It revitalized my spirit like a good multivitamin boosts the body. Once you swallow it, you're hooked. Take some vitamin K with a meal of praise and thanksgiving. Amid the lunch-hour rush that Thursday, I just became one diner helping scores of other diners express the grace of kindness.

Kindness produces a ripple effect, like a stone thrown into a lake. In our fast-paced, technological age, we easily overlook the individual worth of other people. Kindness recognizes the needs of others and helps us meet those needs.

BACK TO THE WORD: KINDNESS/VITAMIN K

"What is desirable in a man is his kindness" (Prov. 19:22). The description of the virtuous woman in the same book of the Bible says, "On her tongue is the law of kindness" (31:26). Who have you been kind to lately? Who has been kind to you?

There is an account in chapter five of 2 Kings of a slave girl who inspired her master's healing. Captured from Israel by Syrian raiders, she worked as a servant to the wife of a man named Naaman. By the world's standards, she was powerless and insignificant. On the other hand, Naaman commanded a powerful army. As a general, he knew the king very well and he demanded respect.

But one blemish haunted Naaman—leprosy. In Israel, he would have been an outcast, but in Syria he rose in the ranks despite his disease.

Now the slave girl could have harbored a grudge. Forced to work in a strange house devoid of devotion to her living God, she could have rebelled. But she genuinely cared about Naaman. Instead of cultivating revenge in her heart, she nourished a heart of kindness.

One day she told her mistress, "If only my master were with the prophet who is in Samaria! For he would heal him of his leprosy" (2 Kings 5:3). She remembered this prophet of Israel who was known as a God-gifted miracle worker. She offered her trust in Elisha and faith in the God of Israel as gifts of kindness to Naaman.

Her humble act of kindness caused a ripple effect upon thousands of people in the land. Her words intrigued her mistress and the mistress told her husband, Naaman. He then told the king. The king of Samaria sent 750 pounds of silver, 150 pounds of gold, and ten sets of clothes to the king of Israel. Many people were blessed by these gifts. The king of Syria told Naaman to go see the prophet and to take the king of Israel a letter of introduction.

Naaman went to Elisha the prophet, and Elisha told him to go down to the River Jordan and dip himself seven times. Naaman's pride almost prevented him from obeying, but his servants begged him to do what the prophet said. So Naaman went to the Jordan, and after dipping himself seven times, his skin became clean. Naaman returned to Elisha's house saying, "Now I know that there is no God in all the world except in Israel" (2 Kings 5:15).

Kindness is an open doorway into the kingdom of heaven. Though only a seemingly powerless and insignificant slave, this girl's words have tremendously impacted the world throughout the ages. Without her, probably few if any of us would have ever heard of Naaman. Whenever we feel unimportant we can just do something kind for someone else. We can take vitamin K and feel better immediately!

GO AND DO LIKEWISE

Let somebody use your grocery store or drugstore card at the checkout line when they have forgotten theirs. Give a discount coupon to a stranger at the mall if you don't need it. Tell somebody where they can get the same great deal you found. Just spread a little kindness.

One day my wife drove home in her 2001 Lincoln LS sedan with smoke streaming from the back left wheel. The car had been difficult to crank all year long, and we could smell gas after every start up. The console air bag light stayed on constantly. The back left window refused to roll up, and a few rain soakings left the car smelling like mold. The front driver side door would not open from the inside and the AC filter was due for service. All in all, we faced a three thousand dollar repair bill and didn't have the money.

But God blessed America! It was "cash for clunkers" month in the land. The Lincoln went from zero-to-sixty mph seemingly faster than Jimmie Johnson's NASCAR racer. It had a powerful V-8 engine that guzzled gas like an elephant sucking up water. It qualified for a $4500 government rebate. We dashed to a Nissan dealer that same evening, knowing that under normal circumstances nobody would give us a plug nickel for that car! The Blue Book value was virtually nothing, so the LS was disposed of the next day. At church that weekend we shared our good news with gladness by telling more than a dozen folks how to take advantage of the clunker deal.

Just as the slave girl was kind enough to share her good news about the Prophet Elisha with foreigners, let us render random acts of kindness whenever and however we can. Perform some drive-up and stop-in random acts of kindness in a drive-by-shooting world. It is good for the soul. What the girl did seemed very small, but it brought Naaman in contact with the God of Israel. Her kindness trumped her powerlessness and insignificance. Do not become discouraged by your limitations. Rejoice in the gifts of kindness God blesses you to bestow upon others. Use what he has given to you right where you live.

KINDNESS UNLOCKS BLESSINGS

A little kindness goes a long way. A smile, a hug, a kiss, an act of friendship, a minute of your time, or a hand of mercy, all go a long way. A listening ear, a word of wisdom, a sympathetic embrace, a bit of food, or a cup of water, all go a long way.

You have much to offer people, like a helping hand, a sign of hope, a gesture of healing, an act of peace, an offer of forgiveness; all go a long way. Maybe you have a little praise, or a little thanksgiving, a little prayer, a little song, or a friendly joke. Be like the servant girl, offer your gift of kindness freely. No money is required to be kind. It's a gift from your heart. And one act of kindness can unlock a multitude of blessings for people.

The slave girl took a great risk because if Naaman had not been healed, she could have suffered severe punishment or even death. But she had great faith in the God of Israel. She took her vitamin K.

There is power in kindness, and kindness is a great stimulus for America today. Let our power expand the kingdom of God. Jesus said to his disciples, "You will receive power when the Holy Spirit comes on you; and you will be my witnesses in Jerusalem, and in all Judea and Samaria, and to the ends of the earth" (Acts 1:8). While others hold the power to destroy and ruin lives, we carry within us the power to uplift, encourage, affirm, and give great joy to others. Use your holy power for good!

REFLECTION/DISCUSSION

1. Have you ever done something on impulse, spontaneously surprising others around you? What motivated your action?
2. A wise woman once told her husband to give five parts praise for every one part of criticism to their children. What did she mean by this? Does this apply to kindness? Why or why not?
3. Name one random act of kindness you have rendered in the past seven days. (If you cannot think of an example, you have gone too long without your vitamin K!)
4. Why does the author compare kindness to a vitamin? Do you agree with the comparison?
5. How does one find time for kindness? Read the description of the virtuous woman in Proverbs 31. Can you find the time in your busy schedule for kindness? How do you do it?
6. Read the story of the slave girl and Naaman in 2 Kings 5:1-15. Discuss the ripple effects of kindness shown by the

servant girl. Is there a current example in your community of someone whose kindness caused such a ripple effect?

7. Naaman's pride almost blocked his healing. How can the pride of both givers and recipients become barriers to kindness? How can you share your kindness with others and respect their dignity at the same time?

8. Make a list of kindnesses needed in your church or community. Go and do likewise.

OUTREACH MINISTRY ACTIVITY

You don't have to go far to share kindness with others. During one church service a pastor spontaneously called all the volunteers who worked in their three-week summer camp to the altar. Dozens of members filed up the aisle. Once they had arrived, he asked the congregation to give them a big cheer for their work. The church celebrated their valuable contributions to more than one hundred children.

This week, take time to visit someone who may be lonely at a nearby rest home or nursing facility. Talk to them, pray with them, and even sing to them. Don't be in a rush, but don't overstay your welcome, either. Ask the Holy Spirit to lead you in what to do and say. Go with a genuine concern like the slave girl had for Naaman. Give that person your heart, love, and undivided attention. If you are nervous about making such a visit by yourself, take a friend or a small group, or ask your pastor or ministry leader for the name of someone who might accompany you. Ask them to give you a few pointers on making the most of your time.

Remember the foreigners among us in our land. Offer your ministry of helps to those who have migrated here from other countries. The slave girl did not allow nationality or religion to impede her kindness. Your random acts of kindness may encourage others to follow suit. They will most likely bless the receiver and surely please your God. "Be kind and compassionate to one another, forgiving each other, just as in Christ God forgave you" (Eph. 4:32).

Vitamin K Stimulus Summarized

Offer your vitamin K (kindness) to others more often in our toxic world. Carry a bottle full of kindness instead of marching out into the world with pills of brutal criticism and scorn.

Kindness produces a ripple effect of gracious good works, like a stone thrown into a lake that produces ripples on the water. Kindness recognizes the needs of others and helps us meet those needs.

Kindness is a doorway into the kingdom of God.

Render random acts of kindness. Do some drive-up and stop-in acts of random kindness in a drive-by-shooting world. It's good for the soul.

JOY-A YUMMY RECIPE

I will bless the Lord at all times;
His praise shall continually be in my mouth.
—Psalm 34:1 NKJV

M ORE THAN TWO decades ago I embarked upon one of the
most joyous experiences of my life. Like a lost son trying to
find his way back home, I eagerly took a trip to my ancestors' land
of origin—Africa. I studied African history in college and developed
an insatiable desire to know more about my heritage. Alex Haley's
1976 classic book, *Roots: The Saga of an American Family,* and the
popular television dramatic series that ensued, only whetted my
appetite for this journey to my motherland.

On Friday, March 6, 1987, I couldn't sleep one minute on Alitalia
flight 814 from Rome to Nairobi, Kenya. I didn't want to eat, see
a movie, or even hear any music during the night flight. At the
crack of dawn, while others slept and first light seeped through
the jet's windows, I threw off my seat belt and walked quietly to
the rear of the airplane. Peering out of a small window, I caught a
glimpse of the clouds. That is all I saw for awhile, but they were
African clouds. Theologically and geographically, where one stands
determines what one sees, and soaring over the motherland I saw

that morning as an African dawn with an African sun and sky. My soul had suddenly tapped into a refreshingly new perspective.

Minutes later, while flying over Kenya, gaps in the white cumulus clouds swung open, revealing vast stretches of mountains, hills, and plains. I knelt and bowed in thanksgiving to God as the landscape unfolded into a kaleidoscope of vibrant greens, browns, earthly reds, rocky tans, and grays. The earth pulsated and as if saying, "Hello, and welcome home." An irrepressible joy overcame me. Spiritually, my soul touched down in Africa while I was still airborne. So I praised God for the dream-come-true opportunity before me.

I shouted hallelujah upon exiting Nairobi's airport terminal, to the pleasant surprise of my Bread for the World traveling partner, Bill Rau. He knew of my longing to visit Africa, and he made the trip happen. He smiled joyfully as I dropped to the ground and gathered the thin, beautiful, coffee-colored Kenyan earth into my hands. I celebrated the goodness of the Lord.

Back to the Word: Joy—A Yummy Recipe

"I will extol the Lord at all times; his praise will always be on my lips. My soul will boast in the Lord; let the afflicted hear and rejoice. Glorify the Lord with me; let us exalt his name together.... Taste and see that the Lord is good; blessed is the man who takes refuge in him" (Ps. 34:1-3, 8).

Psalm 34 is like a pineapple upside down cake. The best part—the pineapple slices, brown sugar, butter, maraschino cherries, and walnuts—go into the cooking pan first and simmer into the cake batter poured on top. After baking, the cake is turned right side up and the fruit mix flavors the whole cake.[1]

This psalm depicts my experience flying into Nairobi. My joy and praise erupted first, even before my three-week journey throughout three African nations. Putting our praise before our blessings is an anomaly. My mid-air exultation seemed upside down, but sometimes the goodness that God bestows must be joyously celebrated even before the Creator unleashes those blessings. This is the order that the psalmist pours out blessings, adoration, praises, and gratitude to God in the first eight verses of this thanksgiving hymn. David gave us his "fruit of praise" with enthusiasm for the Creator's life-giving power and deliverance. "I sought the Lord, and he answered me; he delivered me from all my fears" (34:4). This joy for God saturated the psalmist's heart, and he freely invited others to taste for themselves the goodness of the Lord. "Taste and see that the Lord is good; blessed is the man who takes refuge in him" (34:8).

Such joy shows how much David trusted God. Despite strongholds of negativism, danger, violence, and anger in his world, he constantly kept God's praises in his mouth. We must imitate David in our speech, conversations, thoughts, and prayers. Like the fruit on the pineapple upside down cake, our faith, praise, and boasting in the Lord should saturate our minds, bodies and spirits, and fill us with good things each day of this decade.

David said, "let the afflicted hear and rejoice." The humble, oppressed, afflicted, poor, those with low expectations, seniors, and children are all invited to hear the praises of the psalmist and join in his gladness! All people are urged to experience the amazing fellowship of God's presence.

Joyful Praise Helps Dismantle Evil

With this joyous expectation, David tells us to watch the Lord deliver us from all our fears (34:4). Expectant praise is not easy in our world today, but it helps deconstruct the evil that invades our lives. Joyful praise disarms and dismantles some of the negative forces surrounding us before they level us into the dust. Joyful praise breathes life and strength into us, so we should not wait until Sunday to get our praise on and taste and see that the Lord is good every day.

Remember the Bible story about Paul and Silas offering up joyful praise in the Philippian prison cell (Acts 16:16-31). They had saved a young slave girl from her spirit of divination. That evil spirit was lucrative to her masters, who profited from her fortune-telling. The authorities seized the apostles because of their exorcism. Paul and

Silas were beaten, taken into custody and imprisoned. With their feet clamped in chains they erupted into joyful praise and worship in the darkness at midnight. The point is that we must manage to praise God even in the darkest of times.

Then a great earthquake shook and opened the doors of the prison and the disciples' chains broke from their feet. The shake-up was a miracle that set them free! It reminds us that joyful praise contains heavenly power to shake up our lives and free us from the shackles of evil. Many burdens of life can be lightened.

This is not to say that all troubles and worries are bad. Some woes warn us to take precautions. The threat of a deadly flu pandemic in 2009 caused us to wash our hands more vigorously and to get vaccinated. It is human to feel sorrow and experience fear, yet some fear may be positive. It may keep Californians from remaining in their homes when wild fires close in on them, or keep New Orleans residents from staying in their homes when large hurricanes approach. Some fear is healthy.

Also, when a child dies in an accident or when a Chicago teen is killed in a drive-by shooting, we weep and mourn in pain. We sympathize with the hurts of others. Joyful praise appropriately waits on the sidelines when we are crushed by great tragedies. It allows us to travel through shock, grief, anger, and withdrawal, before joy emerges in us again. But extremely prolonged despair should be avoided. It produces stress, health problems, and spiritual weakness. Excessive worry is destructive, so do not wallow in heartaches too long or you may drown in them. Returning to joyful praise to God is a restorative stimulus helping us regain spiritual and emotional equilibrium in a topsy-turvy world.

Singing Promotes Joy

Joyful praise is an essential part of Christian life. When we shout in worship, we show joyful praise. Hand clapping and gestures of celebration demonstrate our delight in the Lord. Singing praise songs celebrates God's reign and lordship over all the earth. Singing is at the heart of joyful praise, and our praise erupts as we enjoy the presence of God intensely and intimately.

Many characters in the Bible praised the Lord before being delivered from their troubles. Mary, the humble mother-in-waiting of Jesus, faced ridicule for her mysterious pregnancy, but she lifted up her voice and magnified God even in her poverty (Luke 1:47). The prophet Habakkuk praised God (3:17) even though the fig trees did not blossom, no fruit was on the vines, and no cattle were in the stalls. Also, at least one of the ten healed lepers took time to run back to Jesus, "praising God with a loud voice" (Luke 17:15) even before he went to the priest to be declared cleansed of his disease.

The fruit of joyful praise came from the mouth of a destitute blind beggar named Bartimaeus, who boldly called out, "Son of David, have mercy on me" (Mark 10:47). The surrounding crowd tried to silence the boisterous man, but he was undeterred. Without natural eyesight, Bartimaeus threw off his cloak, one of the poor beggar's few possessions, and sprang up to Jesus, saying, "My Master!" He asked for his sight to be restored, and immediately Jesus healed him. Such positive expectations and joyful praise are forces for liberation when we lovingly offer them to God.[2] So give praises of joy to the Lord and expect God's gracious guidance.

GO AND DO LIKEWISE

Do not allow the world to deny you a fruit of praise dessert. Skip the main course sometimes and go for the dessert.[3] Our church holds an annual homecoming service where I invite the members to prepare "scratch cakes" for the homecoming meal. These are home-made cakes, not cakes from store boxes. The congregation responds with scores of home-baked cakes and pies. After worship, I join them in the church dining hall for lunch. While they line up for the main course, I sample the best desserts on the table.

So praise God joyfully even when your pockets are empty, because God will supply your needs according to the riches in heaven. Lift up joyful praise when you are sick in bed, for the Lord holds all healing in divine hands of grace. Joyfully exalt the Lord while riding in your old, temperamental car, because a new car may be coming off Detroit's assembly line with your name invisibly stamped on it by heaven. And do not forget to give God joyful praise on your crazy job because the Lord will see you through and may even send you a better one.

Instead of heading off into the meat and potatoes of our day's toils, let us first eat the dessert of joyful thanksgiving early in the morning. Have some cherries jubilee praise, some double chocolate fudge hallelujahs, some pie a la mode gratitude, some pineapple upside-down cake prayers and singing. Take time to rave and boast and clamor about the goodness of the Lord as a preamble to your day.[4] Magnify the Lord, exalt God's name, and taste the Lord firsthand. Do it the first thing, before anything else.

Lick the Dasher

Years ago, my mother would put all the ingredients for her scratch cake into a mixing bowl and turn on the electric mixer to combine them. She was an expert of the trade. After the batter became smooth and creamy, she turned the mixer off, pulled out the *dashers* (the removable metal attachments that spin around swiftly in a mixing bowl), and allowed me to lick the batter off of them. It tasted so sweet, foretelling how good that cake would turn out when baked.

The Bible commands us, "Taste and see that the Lord is good" (Ps. 34:8). When we do, God allows us to know how good life can be.

"Rejoice in the Lord always," the apostle Paul said. "I will say it again: Rejoice! ...Do not be anxious about anything, but in everything, by prayer and petition, with thanksgiving, present your requests to God. And the peace of God, which transcends all understanding, will guard your hearts and your minds in Christ Jesus" (Phil. 4:4, 6-7).

Praise May Erupt Anywhere!

I will never forget driving down Interstate 95 south from Washington, D.C., in 1988. I left the nation's capital city and headed home to pastor a church in Raleigh, North Carolina.

About one hour into my trip, I pulled out a cassette tape by Denise Williams and flipped it into the car's audio system. After a couple of soulful Christian selections, she sang "All to Jesus I Surrender." I had heard that old hymn many times, but I never heard anything quite like her rendition. That song brought a joyous stream of tears to my eyes.

> All to Jesus I surrender, all to Him I freely give;
> I will ever love and trust Him, In His presence daily live.
> I surrender all, I surrender all,
> All to Thee my blessed Savior, I surrender all.[5]

I had just finished five years of work with an outstanding organization, but I was really not needed there anymore. For weeks, no job prospects surfaced. As the chief bread winner for my wife and two kids, I naturally worried a bit. Nevertheless, I fervently prayed to the Lord and gave God joyous praise for many good years on that job. I thanked God through my troubles, knowing that he would provide.

Eventually, a church in Raleigh asked me to return home to serve them. Therefore, hearing Denise's version of that old hymn set off a one-man praise party on I-95. I played that hymn at least five times, rewinding it again and again. I bounced in my car seat to the beat, shaking my head from side to side, waving my hands in the air, and lifting holy hands of joy to my mighty God. I shouted aloud and wept for joy!

People passed me on the left and right, some wondering if I had lost my mind. While I would not advise you to duplicate my actions as I drove at a seventy-mile-per-hour clip, I do recommend that joy should fill you throughout the course of your day. When the praises go up, the blessings come down. To this very day "I Surrender All" is my favorite hymn. May your joyous surrender to Jesus Christ bear great fruit of praise to God in this decade of promise.

REFLECTION/DISCUSSION

1. Can you recall one of the most joyous times in your life? What happened? How did you feel?
2. In Psalm 34, David gives joyous praise to God before mentioning the Lord's blessings. Does this seem backwards? Does this make sense to you?
3. Have you ever praised God joyously in anticipation of the Creator's goodness? Has joyous praise ever lightened the burdens you feel?
4. What have you learned from your reading of Psalm 34? What help do you find in its words?
5. Do you stay home from church when you are emotionally upset, or do you make sure you get to church under those circumstances? What would you recommend to others and why?
6. Do you practice private devotion time at home (prayer, adoration, scripture reading, music, praise, thanksgiving, singing, etc.)? Is this time a joyful experience? Does this spiritual discipline improve the outlook for your day?
7. When did you last enjoy an intensely intimate time with God? What were the results?
8. Study the hymn "Joy to the World." What does it say about joy? Why is it one of our most sung Christmas carols?
9. What Christian hymn or song brings you great joy when you sing it? Why does it set off praise in your heart?

OUTREACH MINISTRY ACTIVITY

Have your group or church prepare homemade scratch cakes, pies, and other desserts, and take them to a hospital or residential center for the mentally impaired. In Goldsboro, N.C., there is a wonderful state facility for the mentally impaired called O'Berry Neuro-Medical Treatment Center. Each Christmas O'Berry's foundation holds a Sunday Family and Friends Luncheon for its residents. O'Berry supporters provide sweets for the meal. The O'Berry Center Foundation also receives tax exempt charitable donations:

P.O. Box 1157, Goldsboro, N.C. 27533-1157; 919-581-4187. The Foundation's mission is to improve the quality of life for individuals with developmental disabilities who come from the sixty-seven counties in central and eastern North Carolina.

Find a similar place and bless them with your tables of freshly prepared desserts. Many facilities have special meals for Thanksgiving and Christmas. Find out when your desserts would be most appreciated. Bake an abundance of items, plenty for staff and residents. Remember to throw in some sugar-free goodies for diabetics. Let them know that your Sweets Feast represents the goodness of God. While there, join in joyful praises to God. You may ask to take your church choir or a musical group. Let others taste and see that the Lord is good.

Joy Stimulus Summarized

Sometimes the goodness that God has in store for us must be joyously celebrated even before the Creator unleashes those blessings.

Joyful praise to God helps to disarm negative forces in our lives before they beat us down into the dust.

Our joyful worship of God breathes life and strength into us. The psalmist encourages us to "taste and see that the Lord is good" every day.

Participating in joyful praise to God is a preventative stimulus that helps us maintain spiritual and emotional equilibrium in a topsy-turvy world.

Praise is the spontaneous outpouring of our joyful presence with God. The world cannot give us this kind of joy, and the world cannot permanently take it away. It is a gift of God springing forth from the heart of those who intensely and intimately love God.

PART FOUR
TAKE YOUR VICTORY LAP

OBEDIENCE AND ALMIGHTY MOMENTUM!

Then the Lord said to Moses, "Why are you crying out to
me? Tell the Israelites to move on."
—Exodus 14:15

WE LEFT SHAW University's Greenleaf Auditorium all fired up
to march into the streets of downtown Raleigh. We marched
to protest racially segregated facilities in the city's business district.
An ugly crowd of hecklers awaited us, so my sister grabbed my hand
as we filed forward toward the main street, singing and clapping
for freedom.

"Keep your cap on," Delcie said. "Hope you went to the rest
room like I told you. There's no toilet out here." I followed her
instructions because Delcie knew how to lead. Mom and Dad told
her to watch out for me during the march. Only a dozen years of
age, I wisely obeyed my fifteen-year-old big sister as we entered the
city's business district. Scores of hecklers lined the sidewalk across
the street, but police kept us apart.

"Hey, look at those crazy niggers," one burly man shouted.
"Looks like a good coon hunting day!"

"Damn your kind," a woman hollered. "Yawl go to hell...ought to
be glad we let you in this country. Go back to Africa with Tarzan!"

"Don't pay them any attention," Delcie countered. "Nobody's going to hurt you. Just stay in line."

Why were they so mad? I couldn't understand why they boiled with such hate. The heat of their anger and their cutting insults bruised me like a punch from Muhammad Ali, even though no one laid a hand on me.

"Yeah, show us your tails you little monkeys!" a red-faced man shouted from the back of a passing pickup truck while a snarling woman waved a confederate flag from the passenger side window. Then I saw people in front of me ducking. A rider in another truck had blown a big ball of spit from his mouth toward us.

"Are you OK?" Delcie inquired after stooping down toward the sidewalk herself. "It's OK. Just keep walking. We're all together and everything's fine." Delcie was tough for her age. At five-feet, ten-inches tall, she towered over me. She was an imposing figure whose steely strength foreshadowed an army nursing career in Vietnam.

"I hope they don't throw rocks," I said. "That happened one day."

"Hush! Let's not talk too much." She told me to hold her hand real tight and said, "Stay close to me...right beside me now. We'll get through this together." Again I obeyed, finding great comfort in her captain-like orders.

Then in the midst of the march, we sang: "We shall overcome, we shall overcome... for deep in my heart, I do believe, we shall overcome, someday." The music inspired us forward, drowning out the cursing and vile name-calling nearby. The songs made us press on to a higher calling. Nobody would turn us around; not even die-hard bigots worked up into a frenzy.

Nostalgic Segregation?

More than fifty years ago, my parents shielded me from some of the cruelties of segregation. They made me feel safe in a racially polarized society. I would pass from childhood to boyhood and to the youth stage of life where the sheets would fall from the heads of the social oppressors around me. Yet, as a child I enjoyed the culture and traditions of our neighborhood. I savored walking a mile downtown on Saturdays to visit the black Richard B. Harrison Library. Located in an ante-bellum white wooden house, the library hosted scores of eager teenage Negro students. We enjoyed whispering with friends and searching for books to complete our school assignments.

Sometimes we would go to the segregated Ambassador Theater, the only white movie house in town that admitted colored people. We entered by a side door and sat in the balcony, but gee, we had fun throwing popcorn down on the white movie-goers on the main floor. The balcony afforded the best view of the movie screen. At least that rationalization eased the sting of our obvious second-class citizenship. The only alternative to the Ambassador was the all-black Lincoln Theater, more commonly called the "Rat Box."

During the summer, my family gathered around our box-shaped TV set watching a local dance show entitled Teenage Frolics. One Saturday the black teens danced, and the next weekend the white youth took their turn. What a difference in the dance styles. We were excited when American Bandstand, a nationally televised dance show, finally broke the color barrier with a few Negroes shaking and twisting to the latest top-ten tunes. And when the black produced Soul Train dance show hit the national airwaves, Saturdays in Raleigh were turned into dance parties in most Negro homes blessed with a television set.

The Negro community flourished with vibrant events and activities. We treasured the Negro colleges' homecoming parades—Shaw U. and St. Augustine's College. They featured nearly every colored community organization in town with bands, floats, decorated cars, queens, and kings from every nursery school and church. For two hours these ethnic affairs filled the streets with music, laughter, and friendly conversations.

Big Flaws Down in Dixie

By my twelfth birthday, however, I noticed more flaws in good ole Dixie. Serious issues lurked beyond my parents' social safety net. Dr. Martin Luther King, Jr., the civil rights movement, and television coverage opened my eyes to the ugliness in our town. College students from the colored North Carolina A&T State University in Greensboro—only two hours west of Raleigh—began the lunch counter sit-in movement at a Woolworth dime store. In Raleigh, many Negroes had poor jobs, poorly equipped schools, a dilapidated Negro hospital, sub-par public accommodations, back-of-the bus transportation, lower wages for equal work, higher grocery prices in their neighborhoods, slum housing, and slum landlords. The list went on and on. As my teen years progressed, my environment became an insult to my humanity as much as a kaleidoscope of fond memories.

I suffered through the TV editorials of Jesse Helms denouncing Dr. King. Helms intentionally stumbled when pronouncing the word Negro. It always came out as Nig'-gra. Helms built his large eastern North Carolina viewing audience into a segregationist political force who sent him to the U.S. Senate for many years.

Living in the Helms-Strom Thurman South, I soon realized why my dad pulled his car over on the highway and let me and my sister run into the pine trees nearby to relieve ourselves. Few businesses provided restrooms for colored people along the South's countryside. Restaurants would not sell Negroes food, so we carried fried chicken and side dishes wrapped up in neat cardboard shoe boxes and ate in our car.

Breaking Jim Crow's Teeth

In protest, our voices and our feet became animated by years of such indignities. We patiently but methodically filed by segregated downtown stores, hotels, restaurants, and other public facilities. We embraced a biblical mandate: "The Spirit of the Lord is on me, because he has anointed me to preach the good news to the poor. He has sent me to proclaim freedom for the prisoners and recovery of sight for the blind, to release the oppressed, to proclaim the year of the Lord's favor" (Luke 4: 18-19). We knew Jesus said these words just before an angry mob led him to a hill in his hometown to kill him.

So we marched forward. We could not stay locked in the teeth of segregation. We had to knock out Jim Crow's (a name for segregationist laws) teeth. Segregation and discrimination needed a knock-out punch. Carpe Diem! We seized the time, a time ripe for freedom. We knew it, God knew it, and the words of abolitionist Frederick Douglass expressed it: "Where there is no struggle, there is no progress."

BACK TO THE WORD: OBEDIENCE AND ALMIGHTY MOMENTUM

"Then the Lord said to Moses, 'Why are you crying out to me? Tell the Israelites to move on. Raise your staff and stretch out your hand over the sea to divide the water so that the Israelites can go through the sea on dry ground'" (Exod. 14: 15-16).

During one of the greatest events recorded in the Bible, the Lord told Moses to stop praying and to get moving forward! Sometimes we know what to do, but we pray for more guidance as an excuse to postpone moving into the unknown.

As Pharaoh and his army approached, the people of Israel saw the Egyptians in the rear, marching toward them. The people panicked and cried out to the Lord for help. Then the Lord asked Moses, "Why are you crying out to me? Tell the Israelites to move on."

Normally, crying out to God is a good sign. Our ardent prayers for help are indications of our dependence upon God's providential care. This crying out by Israel, however, was totally unnecessary because God pledged to deliver them safely to Canaan. The Israelites were not to rest at their encampment, but to form a line to march and descend to the very shore of the sea and wait there for instructions. Many people today want to return to the 20th Century. They fantasize about the "good ole days" of typewriters, pipe organs, wrist watches, 45-rpm records, twenty-five cent hamburgers and gasoline (per gallon). They glorify the past and hold to worn out traditions. Yet, God has called them to advance. When God calls us forward, the Holy One is already present where we are headed. Be obedient. As a wise New Testament Jewish leader named Gamaliel told the Pharisees, don't get caught "opposing God."

Momentum Builders

Moses raised his rod up in the air and waved his hands over the sea for the waters to divide. Remember, God never moves us to places where we will have to retreat. He has already prepared the way of escape, a path to freedom. Our obedience stimulates momentum from heaven and energizes our steps.

Harriett Tubman, known as Black Moses for leading hundreds of slaves to freedom from the eastern shore of Maryland, sometimes held a gun to the head of an escaped slave to keep him or her moving forward. While transporting them on the Underground Railroad, Tubman quickly realized when they grew weary, fearful, and tempted to stop or return to the plantation. Harriett's gun kept momentum going.

When God has a task for us to accomplish, the Almighty can press us into action through the power of circumstances, events, and people surrounding us. The Creator provides an environment for momentum and success.

The Pinewood Derby

I learned more about momentum at nine-years old as a Cub Scout. My dad helped me build a small wooden replica of a race car for the scouts' annual Pinewood Derby. The big indoor jamboree unfolded at the famous Reynolds Coliseum in Raleigh, with thousands of people on hand watching. Scores of boys entered the contest with unmanned race cars carved from small blocks of wood. The racers rolled down a long, steep declining board onto an equally long but flat straightaway toward the finish line. Many preliminary trials preceded the finals.

My dad was so very smart. A six-foot-four-inch jack-of-all-trades fellow, he knew the maximum weight allowed for the car and possessed an innate understanding of the laws of gravity. My car fell well under the weight limit, so he put BB gun pellets into the wood underneath the car to increase its weight. He strategically placed them so that my car gained MO just when it hit the track straightaway.

Though neither pretty nor aerodynamic, my car contained the right stuff in the right places. Other boys' fancy racers would often pull slightly ahead of my car, but then, on the straightaway, mine took off like lightning! The momentum of the weights pushed my car past the competitors. One after one they fell victim to my roughly hewn red racer. Out of more than two hundred entrants, I made the finals, finished third, and won a small bronze cup. That trophy was like winning the Olympics!

God gives life momentum, and we are to "run with perseverance the race marked out for us. Let us fix our eyes on Jesus, the author and perfecter of our faith" (Heb. 12:1-2). When God's Spirit resides inside of us, that divine power provides momentum to advance.

The Israelites went down to the sea even though they could not see how to cross! God blessed them with momentum. The ten plagues in Egypt convinced Pharaoh to let them go, and now they marched forward by faith, not by sight. Get down to the sea, God insisted. Some grumbled and complained and wanted to go back to Egypt, but God prevented any about-face maneuvers. Temptation would not spoil the Lord's victory.

"No temptation has seized you except what is common to man. And God is faithful; he will not let you be tempted beyond what you can bear. But when you are tempted, he will also provide a way out so that you can stand up under it" (1 Cor. 10: 13). When our foes bear down upon us like the Egyptians, we must not lose heart. Grumbling and complaining betray an unbelieving spirit. Rather, we must courageously and obediently advance.

Holy Timing Moves Us Forward

In 2006, I attended my first writer's conference in the mountains of western North Carolina. I wanted to write a book. Armed with paper and a laptop, I spent a week in training sessions and feverishly writing. After a week, I returned home and wrote for several days, but a clear purpose for the book eluded me. So I stopped writing.

Three years later, God called me to write this book. The Lord poured out the Holy Spirit upon me, set me to writing and endowed me with wisdom. There was a good reason for the delay; I had to know that God was in charge and crafting the book. It would not be completed by human might but by the Creator's power and for the glory of God. After a three-year hiatus, my earlier writings made sense and easily meshed into the final product. Surely, God works in mysterious ways.

Positive forward movement results from obedience to God and from sensitivity to the timing of God. Ecclesiastes reminds us that there is a "season and a time for everything under heaven." God assured the Israelites of safely reaching the other side of the great sea. Pharaoh pursued, but God prevented him from capturing them. Pharaoh's army sank into the sea and perished.

Fear must not threaten our forward movement.

Fear may sometimes be helpful, but more frequently it immobilizes us or sends us off in the wrong direction. Fear makes us hear strange voices of deception and confusion. Grumbling and complaining voices arise. God told Moses to get down to the sea and wait. Moses and the people obeyed. Then God provided a cloud to guard their rear flank and hold the Egyptians at bay. While closing the back door, preventing the Israelites from retreating, God opened the front door. The sea rolled up on both sides forming dry ground for the people to escape.

Except for the resurrection of Jesus Christ, God derived more glory from this signature biblical event than any other in history. God dried the earth below the Israelites' feet, but when the Egyptians followed in hot pursuit, they sank hopelessly into the mud of the sea's soggy bottom. What a mighty God we serve!

Keep your faith, because God can do anything. Don't give up. The prophet Micah wrote about what the Lord requires of us, which is "to act justly and to love mercy and to walk humbly with your God" (6:8). Therefore, move forward, "not by might nor by power, but by my Spirit, says the Lord Almighty" (Zech. 4:6).

We will often be tempted to stay in the same place or to return to forbidden territory. The Devil often strikes fear into our hearts and minds, but saints of God must obediently move forward upon hearing Christ's marching orders.

Get the "Buts" Out

While seated among some Pharisees at dinner, Jesus told them a story about a certain man who sent his servants out to invite guests to his supper. All three invited guests made excuses. One went to inspect a field, another declined due to a recent marriage, and then another purchased five oxen and went to look them over. "But they all alike began to make excuses" (Luke 14:18).

To advance and gain new territory for the kingdom of God, we must get the "buts" out of our mouths. "I would do it, but ...." " "I know I should, but ...." " "I would help, but ...." " "I'd like to, but ...." " God does not want our "buts." Suppose Jesus said, "I really hope for your salvation, *but* this cross is too heavy." No, instead, Jesus marched through Jerusalem, bearing his rugged cross on his beaten back. He marched up the hill of a cemetery outside the city and got nailed to that wooden cross.

The Devil could never defeat the Almighty. Jesus marched forward as far as he could. He knew that through obedience and faith in the Father of heaven and earth that he would overcome the Devil. And Christ's obedient sacrifice provides a path for us to escape the penalty for our sins. Because Jesus marched forward to the cross, we have hope for tomorrow. On Sunday after the crucifixion, God showed the world what power really was all about.

Go and Do Likewise

In 2000 I completed my third year of graduate studies at Drew University, and I hoped to march in the spring commencement. Having worked very hard to complete a one hundred-plus page professional paper required for the Doctor of Ministry degree, I tried for weeks—rather unsuccessfully—to get my work approved by my faculty adviser. He refused to even answer my calls. I knew that the Spirit called me to this three-year ordeal, and my church granted me a month off to complete my paper. Now I waited in limbo, frustrated and confused.

I had gone as far as I could and was unable to get help from other seminary department leaders, so I cried out to the Lord in distress. I detested the prospect of languishing in an academic wilderness like some other doctoral candidates, waiting year after year, sometimes for naught, hoping to get a dissertation approved and receive permission to graduate.

As I cried to the Lord, again the Spirit came upon me. The Lord commanded me to get up off my knees and put my paper and pen away. God directed me to telephone my adviser's student assistant and send a copy of my paper to her. Then I was told to leave the matter with God. Obediently, I did just that. About a week later, the student assistant called and said I had been approved for graduation.

As a boy, I learned to obey my big sister. As a man, I have learned the wisdom of obeying my big God, who can carry us far beyond the boundaries of human capacity.

REFLECTION/DISCUSSION

1. Where were you during the 1960s civil rights battles? Were you protesting segregation or supporting it? Have your views changed since then? How? If you are under fifty years old, which side would you most likely have been on? Why?

2. If you had been with the Israelites at the sea with Moses, what would you have said to your family and friends? Would you have supported Moses or grumbled and complained?

3. Recall your youthful days. What difficulty did you overcome? Who helped you move forward at a critical time in life?

4. What mountain of adversity faces you now? Are you climbing up that mountain or still at base camp? Have you given up climbing and gone back down the mountain, or do you anticipate reaching the peak and conquering your mountain?

5. Have you ever contemplated returning to places and habits that are not pleasing to God? How can you start moving forward again?

6. What is God calling you to do to seize the time and take advantage of an opportunity open to you?

7. Are you an initiator who gets things done, or do you stay on your knees rarely moving forward?
8. Describe a time, recently, that you truly moved forward in faith. What motivated you? Who inspired you? What Scriptures challenged you? How did the waters of adversity open, allowing you to advance?
9. Do you ever make excuses why you can't get something done? Are there too many "buts" in your conversations with God? "I would, Lord, but ...."
10. Has there been too much grumbling and complaining in America in recent years? What lessons can we learn from the story of the Exodus? What will it take for our nation to move forward together?
11. Make a list of your triumphs in life and praise God for those victories.

OUTREACH MINISTRY ACTIVITY

Every fall, high school and college students return to classes. Sponsor a "GO With Almighty MO Back-to-School Day Pep Rally!" During this day of encouragement to students, offer some practical workshops, such as organizing your time effectively and setting priorities, staying focused and completing assignments, managing extra-curricular activities, keeping your private love life under control, maintaining a daily devotional life, and others. Have a couple of good relationship building ice-breakers. Consider breaking up into several small prayer groups each led by an experienced prayer warrior who warmly invites others to share their prayers. Serve a tasty lunch and cap it off with an inspiring, motivational speaker. Give the students tools to succeed and encourage them to move forward with positive attitudes into the school year.

Follow up with your students as the year progresses. Send an occasional note of encouragement or leave an inspiring voice mail, email, or text message. Our church sometimes adopts a nearby school and provides after-school tutoring and other support. Simple gestures may keep many students on the right track.

OBEDIENCE AND ALMIGHTY MOMENTUM STIMULUS SUMMARIZED

God gives us grace and power to march forward and overcome our adversities.

When God calls us forward, the Creator is already present where we are headed. Be obedient and don't get caught "opposing God."

The Holy Spirit provides momentum to help us progress. Grumbling and complaining betray an unbelieving spirit.

God never calls us to a place where we have to retreat, so don't use prayer as an excuse to postpone moving into the unknown.

Get the "buts" out of your talks with the Lord. Quit making excuses.

Because Jesus moved forward to the Cross, we have hope for tomorrow. Christ's obedient sacrifice provided a path for us to escape the penalty for our sins and enjoy the promise of heaven and eternal life.

STRIDES TO VICTORY AND THE HOLY "YET"!

The Sovereign Lord is my strength; he makes my feet like
the feet of a deer, he enables me to go on the heights.
—Habakkuk 3:19

"ARE YOU READY? Get set. Go!"

The teacher's voice rose excitedly as she started the final race of Spring Field Day for the first graders at Longview Elementary School in Raleigh. My son Paul would run the final leg of the relay race for Mrs. Waddel's class. Three classes competed, each entering a three-person team. Every participant would run once around the circumference of the football-sized plateau atop a hill adjacent to the school, quite a daunting distance for seven-year-old kids.

As the second group of runners rounded the last curve headed toward the baton exchange area, Mrs. Waddel eased over to Paul with words of encouragement. "Just do the best you can," she whispered. "Have some fun running. We are so far behind; it would take a miracle to catch up."

Paul nodded OK and eagerly awaited the last leg of the race as the second runner for his class dropped nearly one-third lap behind the leader.

Finally, the last handoffs began.

139

"Go Reuben!" yelled the lead runner's classmates as he rounded the first curve.

"Catch him Michelle," shouted students in support of the second place sprinter.

Then several seconds later, "Run Paul!" Mrs. Waddel said loudly as her students stood motionlessly hopeless by her side. Paul grabbed the baton and took off.

Family Flashback

At that moment, the speed of the race switched to slow motion in my mind. Thoughts of fond yesterdays galloped through my head. I recalled the many weekends I spent playing with my two boys in the parks and school yards around town. I saw myself rolling out a ball and kicking it with them over green fields seemingly designed just for our Sunday afternoon family outings. We would race each other from one goalpost to another. It was our personal family Olympic games. Of course, I gave the boys a half-field lead to even out their odds of winning. Yet, we were all winners. Later, I threw them a miniature football that they would drop, then pick up, and run back at me like a Chicago Bears' halfback. Then I grabbed one boy by his T-shirt and gently tackled him to the ground. Next came the plastic baseball and bat. We took turns hitting and catching.

Mom came along, sitting on a lawn chair while we boys roughed it up. These weekend excursions became our field of dreams, and we loved it.

Then, I thought of the things that I instilled in my son Paul, including the thrill of competition and a love for the outdoors. I knew him inside and out, and I knew the remarkable physical strength he had for his age, his unusual endurance, his love for sports, and his passion and determination to win.

Strides to Victory

Suddenly, I snapped back to the final leg of the school's race. Paul had managed to cut the front-runner's advantage in half as he began hitting full stride. His muscular little legs chewed up the last lap like a galloping deer. He passed runner number two and bore down swiftly upon the leader. With a quarter-lap remaining, Paul strode over the course with intense determination. As fatigue slowed the leader, Paul's feet moved rapidly and confidently around the last curve. He tenaciously bounded over the last one hundred yards of that hilltop plateau in unofficial world record time, according to my estimates.

"Run, Paul. Go! Go! Go!" his classmates shouted, having found new life. "Come on!" they screamed.

"My God! Yes!" Mrs. Waddel blurted out in utter disbelief at the finish line as Paul surged past the leader. She ran and wrapped Paul in a huge bear hug, squeezing the little breath left in him from his winded lungs. I was elated, but I was not shocked. I knew he had the right stuff to run on his high hill.

Likewise, God knows exactly what is inside each of us. The Creator wonderfully crafted us and filled us with unique potential. We are God's masterpieces, "created in Christ Jesus to do good works" (Eph. 2:10). God prepared us to run victoriously upon our high hills—through the challenges of this world. He groomed us to faithfully perform and serve even on difficult terrain and in tough circumstances.

BACK TO THE WORD: STRIDES TO VICTORY AND THE HOLY "YET"!

The prophet Habakkuk told us that "the righteous will live by their faith" (Hab. 2:4, NLT). He saw a vision of judgment upon Judah and punishment upon Judah's enemies, yet he concludes by offering us a triumphant and stimulating prayer of faith and trust in God: "Though the fig tree may not blossom, nor fruit be on the vines; though the labor of the olive may fail and the field yield no food; though the flock may be cut off from the fold, and there be no herd in the stalls—Yet I will rejoice in the Lord, I will rejoice in the God of my salvation" (3:17-18).

Surely, our nation has experienced a season of hardships. Jobs dried up, political fighting erupted, harsh words abounded, wars overwhelmed us, financial markets crashed, tempers flared, and resources evaporated. This crisis had crushing effects on Christians and strained the resources of churches ministering to record numbers of poor and distraught people. More and more citizens lost their homes, their jobs, their cars, and their hope. Hunger in America grew increasingly worse, and so did the length of soup lines at churches and charities nationwide. More and more of the middle class sank into poverty as the rich grew richer.

Can you see a better day? Habakkuk did.

No threat endures forever, and the faithful will endure long past periodic threats to their existence. For Habakkuk, "there was something eternal in righteousness which evil could not destroy, and that those who are righteous would survive because they had that eternal element within them."[1]

This is the vision for the church today—indestructible faith. Though there is evil in our land and world, the church is custodian to the eternal element, the Good News of Jesus Christ through faith. The church is the repository of Christ's victory over death, hell, and the grave. Our vision of victory is one that the world did not give to the church and the world cannot take away. As Christians, we may get crushed by the weights of the world, but we are never destroyed.

We will never be saved eternally by our local, state, or national governments and leaders. Yet, God is still transforming the lives of people everywhere by the power of the Spirit of Christ at work in the worldwide church. This Spirit is the eternal element burning within us that will create spiritual revival and renewal in our land.

The Holy "Yet"

"*Yet* I will rejoice in the Lord, I will rejoice in the God of my salvation"(3:18). Despite hardships and trouble, Habakkuk affirmed his hope by rejoicing in the Lord. His optimism was not fueled by current events and fads, but by revived faith in God's power to restore Judah's people. Therefore, when nothing makes sense and troubles weigh heavily upon us, remember that God strengthens us through our faith. Prayer quickens our faith, and faith helps us take our eyes off of troubles long enough to see the hope of God. "Now faith is being sure of what we hope for and certain of what we do not see" (Heb. 11:1).

There is a holy *yet* in Scripture to encourage our hearts and minds. While people and institutions have failed Americans in recent years, *yet* God will elevate us. *Yet* implies a future time and indicates that there is more to come, that God is still working things out. Habakkuk said, "*Yet* I will rejoice...."

The biblical character Job once said, "Though he slay me, *yet* will I hope in him" (Job 13:15). The apostle John wrote, "Dear friends, now we are children of God, and what we will be has not yet been made known. But we know that when he appears, we shall be like him, for we shall see him as he is" (1 John 3:2). The apostle understood how God transforms us through faith in Christ Jesus. It is a sealed deal, promised to us *yet* awaiting its full completion.

Habakkuk told us to trust the Lord. We have not yet reached our full potential, but God will restore our nation if the church grows in influence and offers justice, love, mercy, hope, and faith to all people. We will become a better America as Christians fully submit to the mighty hand of God and more faithfully connect other people to Jesus Christ. "Therefore we do not lose heart. Though outwardly we are wasting away, yet inwardly we are being renewed day by day" (2 Cor. 4:16). God's response to Habakkuk was a call to wait faithfully for an answer which was eventually to come. At times we may also have to wait on the Lord. We may have to wait in our watchtowers for answers to our contemporary problems, but God will provide answers in due time.

The holy *yet* is a word of expectation. Though the fig tree may not blossom, *yet* Jesus is the first fruit of our salvation. Although the olive tree shall fail, *yet* Jesus Christ is our oil of anointing. Even though the fields shall yield no grain, *yet* Jesus is the final offering for our sins. Though the flock shall be cut off from the fold and no herds appear in the stalls, *yet* Jesus Christ is our Good Shepherd, who redeems us and returns us into the safe keeping of the Almighty.

Running Like a Deer

We can rejoice with Habakkuk because the Lord will make our "feet like the feet of a deer" and help us walk and run on our high hills. Just as my son swiftly strode like a deer over that hilltop plateau next to his school, God will give us swift feet to run over the obstacles we face. If enough people of God keep faith and run their races with patience, looking to Jesus Christ our coach, we Christians will influence our nation to achieve greatness again.

A deer smells danger while bounding along the cliffs of its native habitat. This imagery translates into a person who, in seasons of adversity, is quickened by faith and prayer to run steadfastly in the safe keeping of God. Like my son at the school field, people of God hit their stride best when the heat is on. We go into overdrive and climb the steep slopes of life with confidence, knowing that the Holy Spirit provides a route for us through any dangers. Prayer and faith show us that God will exalt us upon life's high hills. Are you ready for high places? Are you ready to run faithfully upon the high and challenging hills in your day and time?

GO AND DO LIKEWISE

Habakkuk prayed to God saying, "Lord, I have heard of your fame; I stand in awe of your deeds, O Lord. Renew them in our day, in our time make them known ..." (3:2). His prayer is a revival stimulus for the church today. We need prayers today that stimulate our endurance through tough times. Prayer jump starts our strides to victory in this present age. Prayer must cover all of our thoughts and desires and link us to the very heart of God. Throughout the book of Habakkuk, we find the prophet ardently praying while running his race for God.

How disciplined are our prayer lives? How passionately do we desire communion and fellowship with God? Prayer is vital. If we want to stride with confidence over the high hills of life during this new decade, prayer gives us power, focus, direction, and follow-through. Prayer stimulates the human mind and spirit. Prayer allows us to talk to God and listen to God. It is the chain of command from heaven whereby the Creator emboldens our striding.

The psalmist tells us that the steps of good people are "ordered by the Lord" (Ps. 37:23). Too many Americans have fashioned their own plans, their own goals and dreams, and left God on the sidelines of their endeavors. They act like self-contained gods or self-programmed robots. But prayer keeps us connected to the One greater than ourselves. Prayer causes us to seek first God's righteousness, and helps us understand that all things, even the most daunting, can be used by God for our eternal good.

Would anyone allow their children, parents, husband, or wife to walk around the house all day, never speaking and communicating? That would be unbearable and create confusion. Just so, think of the resulting chaos in our lives when we spend hours, even days, without praying to God.

A Ten-Point Prayer Stimulus Plan

T.T. Crabtree offers the following prayer plan for God's people in this present age. I have added one principle to it and consider it a prayer stimulus plan.

Pray directly—James 4:2; John 16:24

Pray submissively—James 4:6-7; 2 Chronicles 7:14

Pray earnestly—James 5:16; Matthew 5:6; Psalm 63:1

Pray boldly—1 John 5:14-15; Mark 11:24

Pray unitedly—Acts 1:14; Matthew 18:19

Pray militantly—Ephesians 6:10-18; 2 Corinthians 10:4-5

Pray continually—Ephesians 6:18; 1 Thessalonians 5:17; Luke 18:1

Pray thankfully—Philippians 4:6-7

Pray responsively—Revelation 3:20 [2]

Pray faithfully and hopefully—Habakkuk, 2:4; 3:2, 17-19; Galatians 3:11 (C. Johnson)

Striding at the Right Pace

One day last year, I went to a park to walk my usual six laps around an asphalt track. A short young woman in a long dress strode past me as I began my first lap. By lap three, I decided to catch and pass her before going home, so I increased my rate of motion. Did I fall prey to my male ego? Maybe.

Into lap number five, I still lagged somewhat behind her short, quick-stepping feet, so I shifted into my Olympic-style fast walk routine. I really wanted to overtake her for some odd reason. Needless to say, by the end of my sixth lap, I failed to pass her. Obviously, she had been walking more often and longer than I, not to mention her being about thirty years younger. She never broke her smooth, steady stride and she never looked back at me. She looked like a deer walking on her high hills, while I struggled along erratically, huffing and puffing in hot pursuit. I wanted to really press on one more lap to win my imaginary competition, but on lap six I grew a bit light headed and thought I heard an ambulance siren in the distance. That brought me back to reality.

"Slow down man, before they carry you off on a stretcher," an inner voice whispered.

Finish your race the best that *you* possibly can. Don't try to run another person's race and at another person's pace. Set your eyes upon Jesus Christ, for he has a pace just right for your life's goals. If you need to run more swiftly, practice running with the Lord every day—not occasionally. Jesus will develop your spiritual stride and stamina. Remember, swift-footed Christian runners have practiced for a long time. Life is more like a marathon than a sprint to the finish, so go at a God-inspired pace.

By the way, make sure that you have already taken your first step of faith to God in Christ. If our ultimate finish line is to reach heaven, we must first take a step of faith toward God. As James said, "Come near to God and he will come near to you" (4:8). Don't chase the wind and run after other people; follow in the footsteps of the Lord and enjoy the trip.

"Since we are surrounded by so great a cloud [crowd] of witnesses, let us throw off everything that hinders and the sin that so easily entangles, and let us run with perseverance the race marked out for us. Let us fix our eyes on Jesus, the author and perfecter of our faith, who for the joy set before him endured the cross, scorning its shame, and sat down at the right hand of the throne of God"

(Heb. 12:1-2). The same Lord Jesus Christ will see us through our race. We will run upon our high hills on earth until, one day, we reach the high hills of the new Jerusalem, leading to heaven and eternal life. Surely, the righteous will live by their faith.

REFLECTION/DISCUSSION

1. Have you ever run in a race or watched a friend run in one? What happened? How did you or your friend feel?

2. How is life sometimes like a race? Is your personal race on track, or have you wandered off into the wrong lane? Did you get a good start or get tired while running? Will you finish strong? What does it mean to finish strong?

3. As you run through life, who have been your best coaches? What impact did they have on your running?

4. Read Hebrews 12:1-2. The cloud or crowd of witnesses describes those saints already in heaven who have run their race with Christ and are cheering you on today. Who might be included in your cheering squad in heaven? Name them. Stop for a moment to thank them for holding a pep rally on your behalf up in glory. Thank Jesus Christ for interceding for you before the throne of God.

5. The Prophet Habakkuk depicts hard times in Judah. Think about recent hard times in America. Were you or others you know affected by the recession? How have Christians and churches been affected by our nation's problems? Who do you know that endured hardships? How are they faring now?

6. Discuss the meaning of the word "yet" in Habakkuk 3:18. Does the word offer you any encouragement? Why or why not?

7. Has prayer helped you run forward in life despite hardships? How vital is prayer to you?

8. Discuss the ten-point prayer stimulus plan. Which three out of the ten must you apply more seriously in your prayer life?

9. What does "running on high hills" (Hab. 3:19) mean to you? How have you been uniquely equipped by God to faithfully serve the present age under difficult circumstances?

OUTREACH MINISTRY ACTIVITY

Many people have not recovered from the 2008-2010 great recession. Some have lost jobs, homes, cars, and health insurance. Bills have piled up. Some struggle to buy food and medicines. Many cannot seem to make ends meet. Their children need clothes, the car needs repairs, the washer or dryer has not been fixed, and they can't even afford a simple haircut or time at the beauty parlor. They may go hungry trying to pay the rent. Their home may be in foreclosure. Even worse, they may be homeless and at wit's end. Many churches and civic groups sponsored people who were dislocated after Hurricane Katrina. Many around us today have been discouraged by the ill winds of recession.

Ask your pastor or a charitable group in your area for the name of an individual or family that suffers from the past economic downturn in America. Have your group gather a list of their greatest needs and determine how you can help. Name your effort "Operation High Hills" or "The Cloud of Witnesses Project." You will be supplying the designated person or family with essentials to get back on their feet. You will become their earthly cheerleaders, pushing them on to victory.

Commit to work with the person/family up to a year. Provide financial, moral, spiritual, and emotional support. Enlist businesses, stores, health professionals, and anyone else who can help provide the support needed. Evaluate their progress regularly. Let your assistance be a catalyst for their renewal, not a crutch that perpetuates dependency. Give them a fish, but also show them how to fish and even how to own their own pond one day. Pray for them and share the love of Christ with them.

Have your group support the Interfaith Worker Justice organization which champions the rights of working Americans (1020 W. Bryn Mawr Ave., Chicago, IL 60660, 773-728-8400). IWJ is a network of people of faith that educates, organizes, and mobilizes the religious community in the United States on issues that will improve wages, benefits, and conditions for workers, especially those in low-wage jobs.

STRIDES TO VICTORY STIMULUS SUMMARIZED

The Creator wonderfully crafted and filled us with unique potential. We are God's masterpieces, "created in Christ Jesus to do good works" (Eph. 2:10). The Divine One made us capable of running faithfully upon the high hills of challenge in our world. So we must put on our holy track shoes for God.

When nothing makes sense and troubles weigh us down, remember that prayer and faith help us take our eyes off of our troubles just long enough to see the hope of God.

Prayer jump starts our run to victory in this present age.

People of God hit their stride best when the heat is on. The Holy Spirit provides a route for us through any dangers we face. When enough Christian believers keep faith and run their races with patience, they will help America achieve greatness again.

Put aside the weights of sin that slow your running. The victory is not to the swiftest but to those who stay in the race.

If the ultimate finish line is to reach the joy and bliss of heaven in this life and beyond, we must first take a step of faith toward God.

BE ENCOURAGED–
WE WIN!

The Revelation of Jesus Christ, which God gave him to
show his servants what must soon take place.
—Revelation 1:1

THE GOOD NEWS today is that Jesus Christ holds our future
in his hands and he is worthy to receive all "power and wealth
and wisdom and strength and honor and glory and praise!" as head
of the church (Rev. 5:9, 12).

The book of Revelation is a reminder that through faith in
Jesus Christ, believers can rest assured that in the end—*we Win!*
Jesus of Nazareth, more than two thousand years after his death
and resurrection, is still the One worthy of our worship because
we have been redeemed to God by his blood out of every tribe and
nation. We have been made kings and priests to our God, and we
shall reign with Christ in God's eternal kingdom in years to come.

Yes, *we Win!*

The apostle John received a vision while banished on the
island of Patmos, a sliver of land located about thirty-seven miles
southwest of the ancient city of Miletus, off the coast of Asia
Minor (present day Turkey). Jesus Christ sent this revelation
to John by his angel. John was exiled on Patmos by Emperor

Domitian in AD 95 because of his loyalty to Jesus Christ and because he would not worship the emperor. Through this divine revelation, John heard the trumpet-like voice of Christ and recorded what he heard and saw in the last book of the Bible.

While in the Spirit one Sunday, John saw a vision that would be a blessing to the Christians who had been arrested, persecuted, dispossessed, oppressed, exiled, and killed during his lifetime. What John wrote about this vision would become a blessing to harried Christians living in the Roman province of Asia Minor as well as to weary Christians living in America and around the world today. Truly, John's strange and wonderful vision from Jesus shows us that God will win the final victory over the forces of sin and evil, and that the people of God will share in that triumph.

If you are not so sure of the future, the book of the Revelation of Jesus Christ is for you. Despite its complexity and rich symbolism, it speaks to the present (in-between) time, full of trials and tribulations. We live in the church age awaiting the second coming of Jesus Christ in full glory. Also, the last book of the Bible reveals things that will take place in the future. John was told to "Write, therefore, what you have seen, what is now and what will take place later" (1:19). It is at the beginning of the church age, after the death and resurrection of Jesus Christ, that we join John's vision in progress. Jesus told John to "come up here, and I will show you what must take place after this" (4:1).

Let us take a look at what John saw in the fourth and fifth chapters of the book of Revelation.

A Picture of God's Throne in Heaven

There was a throne set up in heaven with God sitting upon it and the Creator wearing a breastplate of dazzling red and yellow stones. A glorious rainbow over-arched the throne highlighted by the most beautiful emerald green background. Around the throne sat twenty-four elders in sparkling white robes adorned with crowns of gold. They represent the twelve tribes of Israel and the twelve apostles of Jesus Christ.

Lightning flashed and thunder boomed from the throne, demonstrating the power of God. Seven lamps of fire, representing the Holy Spirit, burned brilliantly. Below the throne was a sea of glass depicting the holiness of God, and in the midst of the throne stood four creatures, all full of eyes and wings and representing all of creation. The creatures never rested as they cried out "Holy, holy, holy is the Lord God Almighty, who was, and is, and is to come" (4:8). And when the living creatures gave glory and honor and thanks to God on the throne, the twenty-four elders fell down before the throne and worshiped God, casting the crowns on their heads before the Creator, saying, "You are worthy, our Lord and God, to receive glory and honor and power, for you created all things, and by your will they were created and have their being" (4:11).

A Crisis in Heaven?

Then the apostle John became very worried and concerned about what he saw and heard in this vision. God held a great scroll in his right hand that was bound with seven seals, and the question arose, "Who is worthy to break the seals and open the scroll?" (5:2). John began to weep because no one in creation was worthy to open the book in God's hand. Then one of the elders told John not to weep because there was in fact one who could open the book.

John then looked around the throne of God and saw a Lamb in the midst of the throne taking the scroll out of the right hand of God. Then the living creatures and the elders again fell down and worshiped by singing a new song: "You are worthy to take the scroll and to open its seals, because you were slain, and with your blood you purchased men for God from every tribe and language and people and nation. You have made them to be a kingdom and priests to serve our God, and they will reign on the earth" (5:9-10). Indeed, Jesus Christ was and is the all-sufficient and final sacrifice for our sins, and his death on the cross paid the price for our place in heaven forevermore.

The four creatures and the twenty-four elders proclaimed Jesus Christ as the Lamb of God and the only one worthy to hold the book of God revealing the victory promised to all believers.

Later in the book of Revelation, Jesus said, "Behold, I am coming soon! My reward is with me, and I will give to everyone according to what he has done. I am the Alpha and the Omega, the First and the Last, the Beginning and the End" (22:12). And those who follow Christ's commandments will have the right to enter through the gates of heaven and into eternal life. If we are Christians who remain faithful to Jesus Christ, we, too, will enjoy the very presence of Almighty God in heaven!

Only Christ Jesus Is Worthy

Who is worthy of a cross hanging on tens of thousands of buildings around the world? These crosses adorn our homes and dangle around our necks, reminding us of our Savior.

Who is worthy of our worship and giving a tithe (ten percent) of our salaries as offerings for the work of God on earth?

Who is worthy of thousands of songs and hymns written and thousands of choirs singing his praises week after week?

Only Jesus is worthy, because through him we win!

Is anybody worthy of worship services in his honor? Is anybody worthy of Advent, Christmas, Palm Sunday, Easter and Pentecost festivals, celebrations, and observances? Is anybody worthy of millions upon millions of people falling on their knees daily in prayer and calling out their name?

Only Jesus!

Is anyone worthy of thousands of chapels, sanctuaries, tabernacles, temples, worship centers, store fronts, and churches that dot the U.S. landscape? Is anybody worthy of a book written about him that is the all-time best seller? And who is worthy of untold numbers of preachers proclaiming his greatness each week from pulpits worldwide?

Only Jesus, the Lamb of God, the Son of God, and Savior of the world is worthy because through him we win!

Who is worthy of thousands of people undergoing baptism in water each year in obedience to his commandments? Who is worthy of billions of people gathering regularly to eat a meal of bread and drink a cup of grape juice or wine in his remembrance?

When we have a clear vision like the apostle John, then and only then will we realize that Jesus is worthy to be worshipped. Because of his oneness with God in glory, we, too, can overcome the world. When we worship, we declare God's worthiness and his only begotten Son's worthiness to be worshipped through the power of God's Holy Spirit. The creatures and elders in heaven fell down to worship the triune Creator—Father, Son, and Holy Spirit—who dwells in unity as one.

Christians need not bow down to any earthly king, leader, president, intellectual, philosopher, entertainer, athlete, rock star, rap artist, country singer, man, woman, or child. Only God is worthy of our worship. No teacher, preacher, politician, physician, or magician is to be worshipped. It is through Jesus Christ, the Son of God, that we win the final victory over death, hell, and the grave. The book of Revelation assures us of a magnificent triumph over sin and evil.

Near the end of the apostle John's vision, he said, "I saw a new heaven and a new earth, for the first heaven and the first earth had passed away....I saw the Holy City, the New Jerusalem, coming down out of heaven from God, prepared as a bride beautifully dressed for her husband. And I heard a loud voice from the throne saying, 'now the dwelling of God is with men, and he will live with them. They will be his people, and God himself will be with them and be their God. He will wipe away every tear from their eyes. There will be no more death or mourning or crying or pain, for the old order of things has passed away'" (21:1-4).

Then God said, "I am making everything new!" (21:5).

Praise the Lord that we can rejoice in a great victory that is promised and assured. After we have endured the world, we will overcome the world like Jesus Christ and dwell in the presence of God forevermore. Jesus was bruised for our transgressions and by his stripes we have been healed. We are already promised glory in heaven. Christ in us is our hope of glory. We are only waiting for the completion of the great reward of our faith.

Jesus said, "Do not let your hearts be troubled. Trust in God; trust also in me. In my Father's house are many rooms; if it were not so, I would have told you. I am going there to prepare a place for you. And if I go and prepare a place for you, I will come back and take you to be with me that you also may be where I am" (John 14:1-3). There it is brothers and sisters! The apostle John quotes Jesus as saying, "Do not worry, believers. I made it back to glory, and you will be with me, too!" Hallelujah! *We Win!* So as long as we have breath, let us praise the Lord Jesus Christ. Let us bless him at all times, and let God's praises forever be in our mouths and upon our lips.

Jesus Christ picks us up each day. He gives us a new song. He heals our sin-sick souls and our broken hearts. He hears our midnight cries. He puts roofs over our heads, money in our pockets, gas in our cars, and food on our tables. He has provided clothes for our backs and beds for our rest. We even have pills to keep our blood pressure down and our ulcers calm. We have aspirin to ease our headaches and shots to ward off diseases. Jesus wants us to live abundantly.

But most of all, Jesus supplied us with his very presence. The apostle assured us that "the one who is in you is greater than the one who is in the world" (1 John 4:4). God in Christ is in us and working through us by the power of the Holy Spirit. Nations will never be perfect, economies will fail, jobs will sometimes be lost, people will rebel against God, crime will continue to plague us, while floods, earthquakes, and fires will threaten us. But in Jesus Christ, we are overcomers. If we keep the faith, we will move on to a greater world of perfect peace.

The apostle John quotes Jesus as saying, "I have told you these things, so that in me you may have peace. In this world you will have trouble. But take heart! I have overcome the world" (John 16:33). Yes, in Christ, we Win!

So let us say like the psalmist, "I rejoiced with those who said to me, 'Let us go to the house of the Lord'" (Ps. 122:1). *Worthy is the Lamb...worthy is the Lamb...worthy is the Lamb! Through him we win!*

The invitation to the Kingdom of God from Jesus Christ is open to all people. Jesus said, "Here I am! I stand at the door and knock. If anyone hears my voice and opens the door, I will come in and eat with him, and he with me. To him who overcomes, I will give the right to sit with me on my throne, just as I overcame and sat down with my Father on his throne. He who has an ear, let him hear what the Spirit says to the churches" (Rev. 3:20-22).

Will you let Christ into your heart today?

If so, you, too, will be singing a new song.

With Christ we win!

GOD'S SALVATION PLAN

(BECOMING A CHRISTIAN AND LIVING IN PEACE)

F—STANDS FOR FAITH. "For it is by grace you have been saved, through faith—and this is not from yourselves, it is the gift of God—not by works, so that no one can boast."—Ephesians 2:8
"Without faith it is impossible to please God, because anyone who comes to him must believe that he exists and that he rewards those who earnestly seek him."—Hebrews 11:6
Express your faith in Jesus Christ as your personal Savior because "The righteous will live by faith."—Galatians 3:11

A—MEANS ALL PEOPLE CAN BE SAVED. "For God so loved the world that he gave his one and only Son, that whoever believes in him shall not perish but have eternal life."—John 3:16
"Everyone who calls on the name of the Lord will be saved." —Romans 10:13
ALL people have an opportunity to be saved if they call upon Jesus Christ.

I—REPRESENTS THE "I" IN sIn. "For all have sinned and fall short of the glory of God."—Romans 3:23 But there is a remedy for our sins:

"For God made Christ, who never sinned, to be the offering for our sin, so that we could be made right with God through Christ."—2 Corinthians 5:21, NLT

Admit to God that you are a sinner and confess, "I have sinned against you Lord. Please forgive my sins."

T—MEANS YOU TRUST JESUS CHRIST to rescue (save) you from the penalty of sin and to guarantee your place in God's family now and in heaven. "To all who received him, to those who believed (trusted) in his name, he gave the right to become children of God."—John 1:12

We trust in the living God "who is the Savior of all men, and especially of those who believe."—1 Timothy 4:10

Put your trust in Jesus Christ now and obediently follow him in all that you do.

H—MEANS RECEIVE JESUS CHRIST IN YOUR HEART. "If you confess with your mouth, 'Jesus is Lord,' and believe in your heart that God raised him from the dead, you will be saved. For it is with your heart that you believe and are justified, and it is with your mouth that you confess and are saved."—Romans 10:9-10

Pray

Lord Jesus, I believe you are the Son of God who was crucified, buried, and arose from the dead. I ask you, Lord, to forgive my sins and save my life. I put my trust in you today for everlasting life now and for the promise of living in heaven one day with you eternally. I receive you in my heart right now and thank you for my new life in Jesus Christ. Amen.

Praise Almighty God for your salvation!

Thank God for loving you so much that Jesus Christ, God's sinless Son, died on the cross for you and paid the penalty for your sins. You are now a redeemed child of God and assured of eternal life. Hallelujah! Now let the peace of God rule in your heart. (Col. 3:15) Go to a Christian church or fellowship and publicly confess your faith in the Lord. "Whoever acknowledges me before men, I will also acknowledge him before my Father in heaven" (Matt. 10:32).

Attach yourself to a Christian fellowship / church

Attach yourself to a Christian fellowship/church that teaches and preaches the precepts of the Bible and that genuinely strives to share God's Word lovingly with all people. To grow as a Christian and bear fruit (produce good works) on behalf of the family of God, you must worship, share your faith (witness to others), study the Bible, and serve the Lord (acts of care and ministry to others). Do these things prayerfully and regularly. Take enough time to look and pray for the right church if you do not presently have one, and do not put this off!

> "And the peace of God, which transcends all
> understanding, will guard your hearts and
> your minds in Christ Jesus"
> —Phil. 4:7

APPENDIX 1

SPECIAL ORGANIZATIONS

Bread for the World

Cape Fear Regional Bureau for Community Action, Inc.

Cumberland Community Foundation, Inc.

Drew University Theological School

Faith Evangelism Curriculum / Lifeway Christian Stores

Fayetteville State University (Chancellor's Scholarships)

Summer Reading Camp for Children / First Baptist Church—
Moore Street, Fayetteville, NC

Hampton University Ministers' Conference
(Early Prayers Scholarship Program)

Hospice, USA

Howard University School of Divinity (Scholarships)

Cumberland County Interfaith Hospitality Network
(Homeless Ministry)

Interfaith Worker Justice

Lott Carey Baptist Foreign Mission Convention, Inc.

Meals on Wheels

N.C. A&T State University Scholarship Program

O'Berry Neuro-Medical Center Foundation

Operation In-As-Much

The Salvation Army

Shaw University and Shaw Divinity School (Scholarships)

Sojourners Community and Magazine

Quaker House Cumberland County

TransAfrica Forum

APPENDIX 2

BOOK PARTNERS

Anderson, Lus A.
Anthony, Booker T. & Teresa
Askew, Jerome & Ida
Banks, Richard A. & Elizabeth L.
Bethea, John & Yvonne
Bethea, Yvette
Birch, Roy & Dorothy
Bradley, Ernest
Brown, W. T.
Brown, Wilbert F. & Lucille J.
Bryan, Clifford & Ruth
Bullock, Doris L.
Burgess, Johnsie P.
Butts, Melody
Casey, John D. & Lois D.
Cathchings, Jr., Haney & Thelma
Cathey, Barbara
Clement, William L.
Cobb, John & Alice
Codrington, Ray & Joyce
Coleman, Oliver & Janet M.

Cummings, Willie R. & Jessie
Cunningham, Doris E.
Davis, Ulysses & Sarah
Dixon, Donald O.
Drayton, Jacquelyn Y.
Dunton, Vernice F.
Edmonds, June
Edmonds, Rachel, Morgan
Edmonds, Kaiymma, Joseph,
    Olivia
Emerson, William R.
Farrior, Helen Hooks
Fleming, Brian & Pam
Fowler, Glorious U.
Fowler-Davis, Marilyn M.
Freeman, Jack & Junetta
Frye, Clarence & Mildred
Gerald, James
Grant, Martha
Grubbs, Vivian
Hales, Romas L. & Theresa J.

Hart, Grace C.
Harrell, Nancy
Headley, Max
Hempstead, Joe & Olivia
Hill, Gladys M.
Hill, Mellotta
Hinson, Pearl Alice
Horton, John J.
Jarrell, Jesse & Mary
Johnson, Delores L.
Johnson, Jacob & Gloria
Johnson, Lena
Johnson, Shirley L.
Jones, Joe D. & Wanda S.
Jones, Tony
Lipscomb, Marvin & Luella
Magby, Shelly & Bessie M. & Family
Magby, Sherrilyn L.
Martin, Hannah
Mason, Raymond S.
McCall, Andy & Maxine
McCollough, Doris J.
McLean, Edithe B.
McLean, R.L. & Madina
McNair, Theresa
McNeill, Jessie
Mims, Leroy
Monk, Michael & Loretta
Montgomery, Gladys

Montgomery, Willa
Oliver, Luther C. & Hattie
Perry, Delois
Porter, Priscilla B.
Purdie, Raleigh & Vera
Quenum, Armand & Jonette
Smith, Ashley
Smith, Bertha
Smith, Effie
Smith, Gene & Ruth
Smith, JoAnn
Smith, Paul & Jean
Smith, Sarah L.
Smith, Travis
Talley, Robin
Thomas, Emma J.
Thompson, Jessie
Villines, Hilton & Dorothy
Walker, Robert M.L.
Williams, J. Russell & Theresa A.
Williams, Andrew & Belvia
Williams, Georgia
Williams, Sylvia & Zarek
Wilson, Mattie
Winfrey, Carolyn
Womble, Christine W.
Worley, Marzella D.
Worrells, Jennie Sinclair
Young, Shenna

*61 Anonymous Partners

ENDNOTES

Stimulus One

1. McGlone, Lee, editor, *The Minister's Manual* (San Francisco: Jossey-Bass, 2008), 162.
2. Boyd, Dr. T.B., III, "I Have Decided to Follow Jesus," *The New National Baptist Hymnal: 21st Century Edition*, 2001, 225.

Stimulus Two

1. *The Word in Life Study Bible,* Nashville: Thomas Nelson Publishers, 1996, 1552.

Stimulus Three

1. Wilson-Hartgrove, Jonathan, "Economics for Disciples: An Alternative Investment Plan," *Christian Century*, September 8, 2009, 25.
2. Haley, Alex, *Roots: The Saga of an American Family* (Garden City, NY: Doubleday and Company, Inc.), 1976, 3.

Stimulus Four

1. Alan Paton, *Ah, But Your Land Is Beautiful* (New York: Scribners, 1981), 210.

2. *The New National Baptist Hymnal: 21ˢᵗ Edition*, 2001, "There Is a Fountain," words by William Cowper, 142.

Stimulus Five

1. Taylor, Gardner C., Shaw University Divinity School 2007 Pastor's Conference lecture, Raleigh, N.C.

Stimulus Eight

1. Fleck, Bela, *Soujourners Magazine*, Washington, D.C., August 2009, 35.
2. Ibid.
3. Green, Michael P., ed., *Illustrations for Biblical Preaching* (Grand Rapids: Baker Book House, 1989), 353-354.
4. "Laughter," *Wikipedia*, the World Wide Web.

Stimulus Ten

1. Johnson, Cureton L., "Thirtieth Sunday in Ordinary Time," *Hunger for the Word: Lectionary: Reflections on Food and Justice Year B*, Larry Hollar, ed., (Collegeville, MN: Liturgical Press, 2005), 185.
2. Ibid., 185-186.
3. Ibid., 187.
4. Ibid.
5. "I Surrender All," *The New National Baptist Hymnal: 21ˢᵗ Century Edition*, 2001, 198.

Stimulus Twelve

1. Smith, Roy L., "Habakkuk," *Know Your Bible Series 3* (Nashville: Abingdon Press, 1970), 47.
2. Holland, W.T., "The Church's Prayer Life," *Zondervan 2005 Pastor's Annual*, T.T. Crabtree, ed., (Grand Rapids, MI: Zondervan, 2004), 260-261.

PW

To order additional copies of this book call:
1-877-421-READ (7323)
or please visit our Web site at
www.WinePressbooks.com

If you enjoyed this quality custom-published book,

drop by our Web site for more books and information.

www.winepressgroup.com

"Your partner in custom publishing."

LaVergne, TN USA
20 October 2010
201580LV00003B/2/P